Aiming for Excellence

Annotations to the NAGC Pre-K–Grade 12
Gifted Program Standards

Aiming for Excellence

Annotations to the NAGC Pre-K–Grade 12 Gifted Program Standards

Edited by

Mary S. Landrum, Ph.D.
Carolyn M. Callahan, Ph.D.
Beverly D. Shaklee, Ed.D.

A Service Publication of
The National Association for Gifted Children
1707 L Street NW, Suite 550
Washington, DC 20036
(202) 785-4268
http://www.nagc.org

PRUFROCK PRESS, INC.

A Service Publication of
The National Association for Gifted Children

Cover Design by Libby Lindsey

Printed in the United States of America.

ISBN 1-882664-72-8

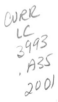

Prufrock Press, Inc.
P.O. Box 8813
Waco, Texas 76714-8813
(800) 998-2208
Fax (800) 240-0333
http://www.prufrock.com

Table of Contents

Foreword vii

Preface ix

Introduction: Standards Development xi

1. Program Design 1

2. Program Administration and Management 15

3. Socio-Emotional Guidance and Counseling 27

4. Student Identification 39

5. Curriculum and Instruction 53

6. Professional Development 67

7. Program Evaluation 77

References 89

Appendix: *Pre-K–Grade 12 Gifted Program Standards* 93

About the Authors 109

Foreword

I am delighted that leaders in our field and members of the National Association for Gifted Students have written this book of standards for programs designed for gifted and talented students. The growth and continued development of our field is dependent upon both the current research and reflective feedback from practitioners and scholars that will chart our course for the future. The best thinking of those who have wrestled with the difficult issues and teach in and coordinate programs for gifted and talented students will help to give focus and dimension to our field as we discuss standards. Standards of excellence in gifted programs are crucial. If our field does not have benchmarks of excellence, some gifted programs will continue to use a random collection of unconnected practices.

The pre-K–grade 12 standards developed and released by NAGC to the field in 1998 have been very well received. This book about the standards cannot be considered an end product or a final work, but rather a work-in-progress that represents our collective attempts to increase levels of quality in the services that we provide for gifted and talented students. This book will add to our current dialogue about high standards in our field and provide our members with the opportunity to evaluate their own efforts and strive toward increasing levels of excellence.

On behalf of NAGC, I would like to thank all of the chapter authors who contributed to the *Annotations*. A special thanks goes to the editors—Mary Landrum, Bev Shaklee, and Carolyn Callahan—for their tireless commitment, and a thank you, too, to Jane Clarenbach, who shepherded the project on behalf of the NAGC national office.

Sally M. Reis
NAGC President
November 2000

Preface

In 1996, then-President Carolyn M. Callahan commissioned a task force of the National Association for Gifted Children's members to study the viability of developing pre-K–grade 12 educational programming standards for gifted education. The 18 task force members were representative of many constituency groups in gifted education, including state directors, parents, higher education faculty, local gifted program coordinators, and others. These individuals also represented diverse geographic areas of the United States. Their work resulted in the *Pre-K–Grade 12 Gifted Program Standards* (Landrum & Shaklee, 1998).

Task force members solicited general input from other individuals from the general membership of NAGC. Contributions from professionals in the field were collected via telephone interviews. Further, a mail survey was conducted of a random sample of the NAGC membership. A collection of state-level documents in gifted education from 41 states was searched for information. Standards documents in gifted education and other fields were examined for style and content. Although the initial standards document contains information from all of these sources, it represents those standards consistently cited across sources as critical to program success. The 1998 document is available from NAGC in a brochure format.

In 1999, the NAGC Association Editor, Dr. James Gallagher, asked the editors of the original standards document to create a guide for practitioners with annotations that would provide a rationale and further explanations of the meaning of each standard. The resulting monograph, *Aiming for Excellence: Annotations to the NAGC Pre-K–Grade 12 Gifted Program Standards*, was designed to increase understanding and utility of the standards. In addition to providing a rationale for each programming standard, we offer benefits, sample outcomes, and potential barriers to success of applying the standards in private and public preschool, elementary, and secondary schools. The authors returned to the literature to document the source of the standards and the scholarly work, which serves as the foundation for each standard.

Introduction: Standards Development

Purpose of the Pre-K–Grade 12 Gifted Education Programming Standards

To assist local school districts in examining the quality of their programming for gifted learners, the National Association for Gifted Children adopted a framework of requisite, or minimal, standards that describe nominal requirements for satisfactory programs. The exemplary, or visionary, levels of performance represent excellence in gifted education programming. These standards may serve as: (1) benchmarks for measuring the effectiveness of programming; (2) criteria for program evaluation; (3) guidelines for program development; and (4) recommendations for minimal requirements for high-quality gifted education programming.

Organizing Principles

Five basic principles regarding programming standards in gifted education guided the development of the 1998 *Pre-K–Grade 12 Gifted Program Standards*.

1. The standards should encourage and guide schools in their approaches to high-quality programming.
2. The standards should provide statements of both requisite program characteristics and standards for excellence.
3. The standards establish the level of performance to which all school districts and educational agencies should aspire.
4. The standards represent professional consensus on critical practice in gifted education.
5. The standards provide statements containing observable aspects of educational programming and are directly connected to the continuous growth and development of gifted learners.

The complete set of standards may be found in the appendix.

Overview of Document

Definitions of Terms

- **Gifted education programming** is a coordinated and comprehensive structure of informal and formal services provided on a continuing basis intended to nurture gifted learners.
- **Gifted learners** are "children and youth with outstanding talent who perform or show the potential for performing at remarkably high levels of accomplishment when compared with others of their age, experience, or environment" (U.S. Department of Education, 1993, p. 3).
- A **standard** is a designated level of performance on criteria that signify programming success (Worthen, Sanders, & Fitzpatrick, 1997).
- **Minimum standards** include requisite conditions for acceptable gifted education programming. These standards make it possible for appropriate practices to occur. The word *must* is used in minimum standards to emphasize that what is stated is requisite for effective gifted education programming. The standards contained within this document assert that there is a need for adequate resources for all students, including differentiated materials to meet the needs of gifted learners.
- **Exemplary standards** provide statements that describe excellence in gifted education programming practice. These standards make it likely that gifted education service will occur.

Format

Each of the seven critical and essential criteria of gifted education programming is the focus of a chapter:

- Program Design
- Program Administration and Management
- Socio-Emotional Guidance and Counseling
- Student Identification
- Curriculum and Instruction
- Professional Development
- Program Evaluation

Within each chapter, the authors provide an elaborated description of the essential criteria. The general discussion is followed by specific consideration of each of the guiding principles. These broad-based beliefs about a given gifted education programming criterion are supported by a description or explanation of the principle and a rationale that provides the current research, theory, and best practice that support the inclusion of the principle in the framework. Following the rationale are illustrations of the potential benefits of applying the guiding principle and potential barriers to applying the guiding principles effectively. Finally, the authors offer sample outcomes that may result from implementation of each of the minimum and exemplary standards.

1 Program Design

by Beverly D. Shaklee, Ed.D.

The development of appropriate gifted education programming requires comprehensive services based on sound philosophical, theoretical, and empirical support.

The belief that any type of gifted programming is "better than nothing at all" is often held out of fear or reluctance for change to improve inadequate gifted education services. Programs that are based on theoretical and empirical foundations are most likely to benefit gifted learners. Band–aid approaches to fixing the inadequacies of the general education experience for gifted learners short-change the development of their full potential.

Rather than any single gifted program, a continuum of programming services must exist for gifted learners.

Description

A continuum of services is predicated on evidence that giftedness is multi-faceted and may manifest itself in many different ways and to many degrees across groups of identified gifted learners. Hence, one program option (e.g., a pull-out program) will not serve all gifted learners equally well. In addition, rather than a single, discrete entity, giftedness is a multidimensional aspect of a child's overall growth and development. Therefore, in order to ensure an appropriate education, a continuum of services should be designed to address specific needs of many different types and levels of giftedness from kindergarten through grade 12.

Rationale

Program development efforts for the gifted require careful planning, development, and implementation (VanTassel-Baska, 1998). Cox, Daniel, and Boston (1985) have documented the need for a comprehensive and continuous set of services for gifted learners that are differentiated according to the nature of giftedness, family, community environments, and age of the child. Opportunities to match needs of students to levels of services, such as cluster group options, special pull-out classes, homogeneous classes, special or magnet schools, mentorships, dual enrollment, and so forth, will maximize learning. Further, providing career counseling, college counseling, personal counseling, and other psycho-social services will ensure that emotional, as well as academic, development is addressed.

Benefits

1. Congruence between gifted learners' needs and learning environment provides maximum opportunity for development in cognitive, psycho-social, and physical areas.
2. Potentially fewer incorrect identifications as behavioral disordered, socially inappropriate, or immature students occur.
3. There are chronological and intellectual peer groups to support continuing development.
4. Gifted learners maintain high levels of interest in learning, motivation, and task persistence.

Potential Barriers

1. Programs designed to offer a continuum of services to gifted learners throughout their educational careers requires more comprehensive planning.
2. One-shot programs (e.g., third grade) or one-size-fits-all programs (e.g., resource room) are easier to manage.
3. Comprehensive programming requires coordination of many school constituencies.

Standards and Sample Outcomes

1.0 Minimum Standard	1.0 Exemplary Standard

Gifted programming services must be accessible to all gifted learners.

- Services are provided to gifted learners in academic and nonacademic areas.
- Services address the diversity of the gifted learner population in both type of giftedness and degree of giftedness.
- Schools establish gifted programming services at all grade levels pre-K–12.

Levels of services should be matched to the needs of gifted learners by providing a full continuum of options.

- Schools establish gifted programming services that are available to pre-K–12 and are specifically designed for the identified needs of the population, including age and developmental levels, as well as any needs identified within the family or community environment.
- Services for gifted students may cross all formats for differentiated programming (e.g., consulting teacher, resource room, part-time, special school, and so forth), but are not limited to a sole program design.
- Services are relevant to the identified needs of the gifted learners and may be evaluated as such.
- Services address student needs in all types of giftedness, including general academic, specific academic, creativity, leadership, and visual and performing arts.

Gifted education must be adequately funded.

Description

In order to develop, support, and maintain a continuum of services for gifted students, programs should be an integrated part of the fiscal management of the local school district. Gifted education programming should not rely solely on external funding agencies, state legislatures, or national efforts on behalf of gifted learners. The funding of gifted education programming should be a part of the continuous budget planning process and should receive comparable support to other such similar efforts within the district.

Rationale

Gifted education programming is often seen as a "stepchild" in educational circles, being among the first of special programs to be deleted from district budgets during fiscal exigencies. However, services for gifted learners are not an addition to their school day; they are the means by which students learn, grow, and develop. When the general education curriculum fails to provide significant curriculum differentiation for gifted learners, it fails to provide an appropriate learning environment for them. Failure to provide adequate funding and, therefore, resources for gifted education programming denies both students and their parents access to appropriate educational services (Purcell, 1994).

Benefits

1. Systematic and sustained program funding allows for continuous progress.
2. Adequate funding promotes growth and evaluation of programming efforts.
3. Sustained funding allows for continuity between and among program services.
4. Sustained funding allows for long-term strategic planning.
5. Sustained funding allows students to have the opportunity to be appropriately served throughout pre-K–12, thus increasing potential areas of development.
6. Sustained funding allows teachers, parents, advocates, and students to focus their efforts on long-term development, rather than on short-term funding enterprises.

Potential Barriers

1. Administrators may view gifted programming as "add-on," rather than integrated with other educational programming.
2. Some local districts look only to state funding or legislative services, such as the federal Javits Program, for funding. Such funding presumes that the education of gifted learners is not part of the overall educational delivery system in the district.

Standards and Sample Outcomes

2.0 Minimum Standard	2.0 Exemplary Standard

Gifted education funding should be equitable compared to the funding of other local programming.

- The annual budget for the school district includes funding designated specifically for gifted education programming.
- States and schools provide continuous funding for gifted education programming that is comparable to other educational efforts of similar size and scope.

Gifted education programming must receive funding consistent with the program goals and sufficient to adequately meet them.

- Systematic planning and goal setting for the continuum of gifted education services provided is part of the long-term planning of the state and school district.
- Funding consistent with the program goals is such that goals can be achieved without the addition of external funding, which could be seen as supplemental, not essential, funding.
- Funding is specific to the continuum of gifted education services provided by the school and district.
- Services are not denied to any number of students, or to gifted learners within a particular domain of giftedness, because of lack of funding.

Gifted education programming must evolve from a comprehensive and sound base.

Description

While there are variations in definitions of giftedness, gifted education programming must be developed with a philosophical base that reflects the values and beliefs of the community. Further, this base is designed not only to mirror the values of the community at large, but also the specific needs of the identified population of gifted learners. Where possible, the base is constructed from a research perspective that determines the parameters of established and "best" practices in the field. When specific research is not available, informed experts with an established record in the field should be consulted.

Rationale

Gifted education programming must be interrelated with general education programming. Programming must be designed from both a theoretical and empirical perspective (i.e., research that supports particular designs or practices with gifted learners) and a practical perspective (i.e., resources available). In addition, such programs should reflect knowledge of gifted learners' development, appropriate forms of assessment, evaluation, and the interrelationship of differentiated curriculum and instructional practices (Callahan, Landrum, & Hunsaker, 1988; Davis & Rimm, 1998; Gallagher & Gallagher, 1994).

Benefits

1. Comprehensive programming provided from a sound base that includes philosophical, theoretical, empirical, and practical knowledge of gifted children has the potential to provide an optimum education for gifted students.
2. Informed practitioners are most likely to be successful facilitators of learning for gifted students.
3. Programs that are carefully and thoughtfully designed provide further avenues of learning and research and provide stakeholders with substantial data on the effectiveness of the program in meeting the established goals and identified needs of students. This, in turn, provides the opportunity for sustainable resources for gifted education programming.

Potential Barriers

1. Program designs that have not been revised in several years often do not reflect consideration of current knowledge.
2. Lack of access to professional libraries, conferences, and consultants who share advice on current research, and theoretical understandings limits the thinking of program developers.

Standards and Sample Outcomes

3.0 Minimum Standard	3.0 Exemplary Standard

Gifted education programming must be submitted for outside review on a regular basis.

- Gifted education programming is reviewed internally and externally a minimum of once every three years.

Gifted education programming should be planned as a result of consultation with informed experts.

- Consultation takes many forms, including direct personal contact, Internet access, and/or the result of reviewing the research literature in gifted education.
- Programming is designed in consultation with informed experts and exemplifies best practices in the field.
- An audit of the program will find direct links between informed practice, consultation with experts, and knowledge of the research base in the field.

3.1 Minimum Standard	3.1 Exemplary Standard

Gifted programming must be guided by a clearly articulated philosophy statement and accompanying goals and objectives.

- Programming documents, including a clearly articulated philosophy statement, goals, and objectives, are developed and updated to reflect a current mission and intended outcomes.
- The program activities are consistent with intended program goals and objectives.

The school or school district should have a mission/philosophy statement that addresses the need for gifted education programming.

- Duly constituted mission statements and policies of the governing body of a school or school district specifically recognize and address the need for gifted education programming.
- Educational documents containing the gifted education programming philosophy, goals, and objectives are readily distributed.
- Programming documents are publicly acknowledged, supported, and disseminated by school and district personnel.

Standards and Sample Outcomes continued

3.2 Minimum Standard	3.2 Exemplary Standard
A continuum of services must be provided across grades pre-K–12.	*A comprehensive pre-K–12 program plan should include policies and procedures for identification, curriculum and instruction, service delivery, teacher preparation, formative and summative evaluation, support services, and parent involvement.*
• Program documents provide specific evidence of a continuum of services for gifted learners from the onset of schooling until exiting that demonstrates a best fit for all developmental stages.	• Exemplary programming is characterized by the above elements, which are described in documents readily accessible to all stakeholders, systematically implemented, and observable in practice. • Exemplary programming includes the collection of sufficient information to evaluate the effectiveness of educational programming in meeting the needs of diverse gifted learners.

Gifted education programming services must be an integral part of the general education day.

Description

Gifted learners are not just gifted for a specific time each day or week. Hence, services for gifted learners are a required part of their total educational environment in order for maximum learning to take place. Programming options that are systematic and sustainable must be provided on a regular basis during the regular school day.

Rationale

The majority of gifted learners spend as much as 50% of their time working with curriculum that they have already mastered (Reis, Burns, & Renzulli, 1992). Further, most regular classroom teachers make few, if any, provisions for gifted learners (Archambault, Westberg, Brown, Hallmark, Zhang, & Emmons, 1993; Purcell, 1994; U.S. Department of Education, 1993). This means that gifted students may spend half of their academic career working well below their abilities. Providing differentiated curriculum opportunities that are regular responses to learners' needs during the school day and access to challenging curriculum in flexible and varied settings are critical for gifted learner achievement.

Benefits

1. The ultimate benefit for serving gifted learners throughout their school day is sustained and prolonged academic engagement (Delcourt, Loyd, Cornell, & Goldberg, 1994).
2. Appropriate learning experiences have the potential to increase motivation for learning and decrease patterns of underachievement (Shaklee, 1997).

Potential Barriers

1. Teachers and administrators in general education have not been made aware of the research, pedagogy, and training necessary to provide differentiated services.
2. Extensive support and professional development provided to all teachers who serve gifted learners are time and cost intensive.
3. Policies that mandate certain patterns of grouping (e.g., heterogeneous grouping only) may inadvertently send messages to teachers that deter from providing flexible patterns of instruction that are beneficial to gifted learners.
4. Administrators and teachers who are not aware of the educational needs of gifted learners or presume that gifted education is elitist may create barriers to a full range of services.

Standards and Sample Outcomes

4.0 Minimum Standard

Gifted education programming should be articulated with the general education program.

- General education programming and gifted education programming are examined for congruency and areas in which suitable differentiation can be developed.

4.0 Exemplary Standard

Gifted services must be designed to supplement and build on the basic academic skills and knowledge learned in regular classrooms at all grade levels to ensure continuity as students progress through the program.

- A curriculum audit is conducted to determine where, when, and how the basic academic skills and knowledge are delivered in the general curriculum in order to adapt and modify curriculum and instruction for gifted learners in advance.
- Gifted education programming consists of educational experiences that capitalize on core knowledge, extend student learning, and apply basic and advanced academic skills.

4.1 Minimum Standard

Appropriate educational opportunities must be provided in the regular classroom, resource classroom, separate, or optional voluntary environments.

- Assessment data is used to match placement decisions and curricular differentiation options to assessed level of needs.
- Organizational obstacles, including the scheduling of staff and courses, do not hinder placement of students in appropriate services.

4.1 Exemplary Standard

Local school districts should offer multiple service delivery options as no single service should stand alone.

- Educational services are provided through a variety of service delivery options that match identified student needs, age, and developmental levels.
- Service delivery includes acceleration and enrichment options.
- Service delivery options are varied in order to accommodate different types and degrees of giftedness.

Flexible grouping of students must be developed in order to facilitate differentiated instruction and curriculum.

Description

Flexible grouping provides favorable results for gifted students (Gallagher & Gallagher, 1994). When teachers use multiple and varied arrangements for classroom instruction, gifted learners can be grouped according to interest, learning style, intellectual ability, achievement, or other aspects of the learner profile depending on the purpose of instruction. Individualized, small-group, and occasionally whole-group instruction can be used in a flexible arrangement. No single grouping pattern should be used as the sole method of instruction.

Rationale

Flexible grouping for instruction provides the teacher with a variety of ways to meet the needs of classroom students. It can provide an opportunity for gifted learners to interact with one another so that they can be stimulated by their intellectual peers. It may also provide opportunities for these learners to be with peers with similar interests or learning styles when appropriate.

Benefits

1. Able learners benefit from accelerated curricular options.
2. Advanced learners benefit greatly from curriculum that is adapted to broaden and deepen their knowledge and understanding.
3. Advanced, average, and struggling students profit from grouping patterns that adjust the curriculum to the level of the group.
4. Gifted children benefit by having an intellectual, as well as social, peer group.
5. Flexible grouping calls for diagnostic and prescriptive practices.

Potential Barriers

1. The greatest potential barrier to flexible grouping patterns is the misidentification of flexible grouping as tracking by administrators who do not understand the difference.
2. Advocates of heterogeneous classrooms maintain that classroom teachers can be effective in differentiating instruction for all children in the classroom. However, research documents that, without intensive training, regular classroom teachers provide very little appropriate differentiation for gifted learners in the classroom (Archambault et al., 1993; Westberg, Archembault, Dobyns, & Slavin, 1993).
3. One frequently used grouping practice, cooperative learning, has little benefit for gifted learners without the use of specific curricular adaptations (Robinson, 1997).

Standards and Sample Outcomes

5.0 Minimum Standard	5.0 Exemplary Standard

The use of flexible grouping of gifted learners must be an integral part of gifted education programming.

Gifted learners should be included in flexible grouping arrangements in all content areas and grade levels to ensure that gifted students learn with and from intellectual peers.

- Documentation and examples exist to guide the use of flexible grouping patterns within various classroom settings.
- The composition of instructional groups remains fluid, allowing for changes in students' needs due to strengths and weaknesses.
- Teachers are encouraged to make use of dynamic and flexible grouping patterns that are congruent with the purposes of instruction and needs of the learner.

- Systematic and continuous provisions are made to pre-K–12 for flexible grouping that allows gifted learners to interact with one another across grade levels and across disciplines. The groups may be within class, across class, or across grade level groupings.
- The grouping pattern can be identified and linked directly to the instructional needs of the gifted learner, including, but not limited to, ability, performance, psycho-social, or physical needs.

Policies specific to adapting and adding to the nature and operations of the general education program are necessary for gifted education.

Description

While policies alone will not guarantee that gifted learners will receive an appropriate education, historically, without such support at the federal, state, and local levels, little systematic service has been provided to gifted learners (U.S. Department of Education, 1993). Policies set the direction for a school district, establish the parameters of fiscal planning and spending, and establish guidelines for services to gifted learners.

Rationale

School policies, which are generally derived from legislation typically tied to funding, set the priorities for teachers and administrators in terms of curriculum delivery, grouping practices, instructional practices, assessment, and identification. Policies also address related issues including early entrance, grade skipping, and dual enrollment. Having well-designed, established, and approved policies in place makes a public statement regarding the commitment a district has to its gifted learners and provides an avenue for parents to address their concerns.

Benefits

1. States that have strong public policies like mandates for service of gifted learners are more likely to continue to provide service even during tight fiscal times (Purcell, 1994).
2. Policy provides a framework for decision making and resource allocation.
3. Policy provides direct support for services and a means by which gifted programming services can be evaluated.
4. Policy provides parents a means to address the needs of gifted learners.
5. Policy documents provide a means by which programming services may be evaluated when determining whether policies have been met.

Potential Barriers

1. Policies put into place without corresponding financial or other resource support can be easily ignored or dismissed.
2. Administrators, teachers, and parents may not be aware of the policies that affect gifted learners, particularly as time elapses and new personnel replace old.
3. All too often, a policy exists on paper only and is not an active part of program planning and delivery.
4. Policies may be based on critical incidents or political power rather than sound theory or research.
5. Policies that are developed to assist one group of learners may inhibit others' learning opportunities, particularly those that limit options for students.

Standards and Sample Outcomes

6.0 Minimum Standard	6.0 Exemplary Standard
Existing and future school policies must include provisions for the needs of gifted learners.	*Gifted education policies should exist for at least the following areas: early entrance, grade skipping, ability grouping, and dual enrollment.*
• Policies on grouping, early entrance, grading, textbook selection, testing, and so forth should reflect appropriate responses to the learning needs of gifted learners. • Policies are reviewed with all staff on a regular basis.	• Policies that are supported by the research literature in gifted education are documented through state and local school policy, meet the minimum standards criteria (Landrum & Shaklee, 1998), and include the above areas. • Policy documents are reviewed and revised to ensure compliance with the current literature in the field of gifted education.

2 Program Administration and Management

By Mary S. Landrum, Ph.D., Gloria L. Cox, and Mary Evans

Appropriate gifted education programming must include the establishment of a systematic means of developing, implementing, and managing services.

There must be an organized and comprehensive plan for designing, executing, coordinating, and revising services for gifted learners. This plan must be administered by personnel that has appropriate expertise in gifted education to develop policies and leadership skills for administering programming options. Although the gifted education programming must be considered independent of other school programs, related services must be fully integrated with total school programming.

Appropriately qualified personnel must direct services for the education of gifted learners.

Description

Effective gifted programming depends on the leadership of individuals with knowledge of the theory and research in gifted education and the skills in decision making and in the administration of educational programming.

Rationale

Research findings indicate that persons without training in gifted education are ineffective in meeting the particular educational needs of gifted learners (Tomlinson, Tomchin, Callahan, Adams, Pizzat-Tinnin, Cunningham, Moore, Lutz, Roberson, Eiss, Landrum, Hunsaker, & Imbeau, 1994), suggesting that there is a knowledge base and specific competencies unique to gifted education. Effective gifted education programming begins with a strong administrator who is an advocate for gifted education. The administrator must be able to describe the needs and characteristics of gifted learners, as well as elicit support from the local school district and community at large (Delcourt & Evans, 1994). Untrained person(s) with the primary responsibility for administering and managing gifted programming must have access to developing the requisite knowledge and skills (Delcourt & Evans). Staff development on the special needs of gifted learners is essential for all staff members. Teachers, for example, need to be aware of both the needs and the various options available for meeting those needs.

Benefits

1. Appropriately trained administrators are able to guide others in understanding the pedagogy associated with the field at both the district-wide administration level and the teacher level.
2. Trained personnel implement best practices in the field of gifted education within the school district.
3. Program administration and management is more likely to be consistent with the empirical base from the field of gifted child education when led by a knowledgeable professional.

Potential Barriers

1. Access to training in the specialized field of gifted education is often not readily available, thereby limiting the leadership candidate pool.
2. Persons with specialized training in gifted child education might be perceived as having a limited vision of the school population and educational programming.

Standards and Sample Outcomes

The designated coordinator of gifted education programming must have completed coursework or staff development in gifted education and display leadership ability to be deemed appropriately qualified.

The designated gifted programming coordinator must have completed a certification program or advanced degree program in gifted education.

- The coordinator is working toward obtaining certification or licensure in gifted education.
- The coordinator is engaged in recognized professional development activities in gifted education (e.g., institutes, NAGC Academies).

- The gifted education programming coordinator maintains current certification or licensure in gifted education at local or state levels.
- The coordinator is engaged in professional development in the area of gifted education that reflects the current knowledge base and best practices that extend beyond the initial certification/licensure in gifted education
- The coordinator of gifted education programming possesses an advanced degree in gifted education.

Gifted education programming must be integrated into the general education program.

Description

The separate and unequal treatment of gifted education is often due to the isolation of those services from the general school program. Gifted education programming must be a part of the fabric of the school district's general education plan and must make a meaningful contribution to the total school program.

Rationale

The integration of gifted education programming into the general education programming promotes the exchange of ideas and pedagogy to enhance learning for all students. Therefore, all educational programs benefit from the integration of gifted education into the entire school program, for example, through improved communication (Tomlinson, Coleman, Allan, Udall, & Landrum, 1996) and overall enhanced classroom instruction (Purcell & Leppien, 1998). These positive spill-over effects of gifted programming result from the view that the integrated gifted education programming services are coordinated, rather than extra, services (Renzulli & Reis, 1991; Kirschenbaum, Armstrong, & Landrum, 1999).

Benefits

1. The program and, therefore, personnel, curriculum, and students, are connected, rather than disjointed, from the district-wide educational programs.
2. Gifted education programming is a collaborative effort.
3. Gifted education services can have positive spill-over effects for the overall school program.

Potential Barriers

1. Existing separate programs may feel threatened by efforts to integrate.
2. Effective integration may not happen if it is interpreted as meaning that gifted programming can be done by anyone regardless of background and training.
3. Parents, students, and leaders of gifted students fear that gifted education programming is diluted when integrated with general education.

Standards and Sample Outcomes

2.0 Minimum Standard	2.0 Exemplary Standard
The gifted education program must create linkages between general education and gifted education at all levels.	*Responsibility for the education of gifted learners is a shared one requiring strong relationships between the gifted education program and general education school-wide.*

2.0 Minimum Standard

- Staff from general education and gifted education plan educational programming for gifted learners that is integrated with the core school curricula, but is appropriately differentiated.
- The general education programs and gifted programming in visual and performing arts work together to identify gifted learners and develop appropriate differentiated services.
- School administrators at every level and across all areas of administration are involved in decision making that reflects and supports gifted education programming (e.g., staffing, budget, student grouping formats, scheduling, and so forth).

2.0 Exemplary Standard

- The gifted education and general education staffs demonstrate shared responsibility for service delivery.
- Building administrators are actively involved in the planning, implementation, and evaluation of gifted education programming.
- Evaluation of school staff includes specific reference to meeting the needs of all learners, including the gifted, and staff are held accountable to those outcomes.

Gifted education programming must include positive working relationships with constituency and advocacy groups, as well as with compliance agencies.

Description

Gifted education programming must reflect collaboration and alignment with the major educational agencies and stakeholder groups at the district, regional, state, and national levels. Within the school district, the leadership for gifted education programming must work collaboratively with teachers, administration, parents, and the community. The gifted education programming also must be in compliance with local, state, and national policies and standards.

Rationale

If gifted child education strives to build bridges with general education, then the programming must involve the major educational constituency and advocacy groups. Further, the programming must be in alignment with all compliance issues at all levels. Most importantly, effective gifted education services should reflect standards for quality education and then gifted education in particular (Tomlinson et al., 1996).

Benefits

1. Positive relationships among leaders of teacher, parent, and other administrator groups promote advocacy for gifted programming services.
2. Alignment of gifted education programming with educational standards and compliance with policy provides program stability and consistency.
3. Gifted education programming that reflects standards of excellence from educational agencies other than those in gifted education have greater support and a wider range of acceptance from a broad group of professionals.

Potential Barriers

1. The programming leadership must be able to integrate multiple viewpoints into policy, procedures, and decision making without watering down their core meaning.
2. Every group has its own agenda, and building consensus from competing agendas is often difficult.

Standards and Sample Outcomes

3.0 Minimum Standard	3.0 Exemplary Standard

Gifted programming staff must establish ongoing parent communication.

The gifted education programming staff should facilitate the dissemination of information regarding major policies and practices in gifted education (e.g., student referral and screening, appeals, informed consent, student progress, etc.) to school personnel, parents, community members, etc.

- Information about the administration and management of gifted education services and policies within the local school district are disseminated in writing to parents, and there are ample opportunities for oral information sharing.
- Parents have the opportunity to share issues and concerns regarding the administration and management of gifted education programming at the local level in a nonthreatening atmosphere.

- Information about programming administration, management, and policies is disseminated to parents in a variety of formats.
- Parents have input into the evolution of the gifted education programming services provided at the local level.
- Dissemination about programming is distributed to the community (e.g., civic groups, business leaders) in an effort to solicit support for mentorships, activity sponsorship, and so forth.

3.1 Minimum Standard	3.1 Exemplary Standard

Gifted programs must establish and use an advisory committee that reflects the cultural and socioeconomic diversity of the school or school district's total student population and includes parents, community members, students, and school staff members.

Parents of gifted learners should have regular opportunities to share input and make recommendations about program operations with the gifted programming coordinator.

- An advisory group for gifted education is used to provide input into local decision making regarding programming.

- A parent advisory committee for gifted education that adequately represents diversity within the total population of the community should meet regularly with a specific agenda for systematic review and recommendations.

3.2 Minimum Standard	3.2 Exemplary Standard
Gifted education programming staff must communicate with other on-site departments, as well as other educational agencies vested in the education of gifted learners (e.g., other school districts, school board members, state departments of education, intermediate educational agencies, etc.).	*The gifted education program should consider current issues and concerns from other educational fields and agencies regarding gifted programming decision making on a regular basis.*

- Gifted education personnel are provided release time to participate on local, regional, and statewide educational committees and consortia in order to provide a voice for gifted education.

- Gifted education personnel regularly review the issues being debated across the school district and become part of these deliberations.
- Essential school committees have representation from gifted education.
- School committee members have current understanding of gifted education issues currently under review.

Requisite resources and materials must be provided to support the efforts of gifted education programming.

Description

Gifted education services must be supported by materials and resources not typically included in grade-level acquisitions. Often, these resources are different from those provided through general education initiatives. For example, personnel require specialized training that is not typically offered in standard professional development efforts. Further, traditional curricula are sometimes inappropriate for gifted learners, resulting in a need for out-of-grade-level materials.

Rationale

Most curricular and instructional materials used in pre-K–12 education are developmentally appropriate for the average learner on a given grade level. However, these materials have limited, if any, value to the gifted learner given his or her particular developmental characteristics and consequent educational needs. Research has shown that, unfortunately, teachers typically use age-appropriate instructional materials and strategies rather than differentiated resources (Westberg et al., 1993). Therefore, supplemental resources must be acquired in order to support the differentiated educational experiences developed specifically for gifted learners.

Benefits

1. The gifted education services are supported with resources and materials that are responsive to the advanced conceptual and processing abilities of the able learner.
2. When funds for appropriate resources are included in school budgets, requisite materials are more likely to be available.

Potential Barriers

1. Decision-making groups might view requests for additional gifted education program resources as elitist.
2. There is a hesitance among funding agents to support specific programming or resources for a narrow portion of a school population such as gifted learners.
3. Instructional materials that are viewed as separate from those used in general education programming might be perceived to be a low priority.

Standards and Sample Outcomes

4.0 Minimum Standard	4.0 Exemplary Standard

Resources must be provided to support program operations.

A diversity of resources (e.g., parent, community, vocational, etc.) should be available to support program operations.

- Gifted education programming has an allotment of resources that provides for at least a satisfactory operation of available program options.
- Resources for gifted child education are included in the general education school budget.
- The diversity and degree of gifted education programming is not thwarted by inadequate resources, especially funding and personnel with expertise.

- Gifted education programming is adequately funded through local and state budgets.
- Community and parent resources have been tapped for appropriate support, particularly expertise and mentorship support.
- Community resources are provided to supplement school staff when needed to provide the appropriate level of challenge in academic and nonacademic areas for gifted learners.

4.1 Minimum Standard	4.1 Exemplary Standard

Technological support must be provided for gifted education programming services.

Gifted education programming should provide state-of-the-art technology to support appropriate services.

- Technology is available to gifted learners as a tool for learning.
- Both academic and nonacademic subject areas are infused with appropriately challenging technology applications.

- Gifted education services include those delivered through advanced technology (e.g., distance education courses, etc.).
- Advanced technologies in the visual and technical arts are provided in order to appropriately challenge gifted learners in this domain with complexity of learning in the arts.

Standards and Sample Outcomes continued

4.2 Minimum Standard	4.2 Exemplary Standard

The library selections must reflect a range of materials including those appropriate for gifted learners.

- Ongoing library acquisitions reflect the different needs of gifted learners.
- Library resources adequately cover the diverse advanced academic and nonacademic interests of gifted learners.

The acquisition plan for purchasing new materials for the schools should reflect the needs of gifted learners.

- The annual plan for materials acquisition includes an allotment for gifted education programming.
- Instructional materials acquisitions reflect support for differentiated curricular and instructional options in all academic areas, as well as the visual and performing arts.

3 Socio-Emotional Guidance and Counseling

by Helen L. Nevitt, Ph.D.

Gifted education programming must establish a plan to recognize and nurture the unique socio-emotional development of gifted learners.

Awareness of the socio-emotional needs specific to gifted learners and recognition of best practices for proactive counseling are essential to the full development of these students. Gifted education programming must include an educational plan containing the appropriate services necessary for nurturing the socio-emotional needs of all gifted learners.

Gifted learners must be provided with differentiated guidance efforts to meet their unique socio-emotional development.

Description

Although gifted learners are typically as well adjusted as other children (Colangelo, 1997; Kerr, 1991; Robinson & Noble, 1991; Silverman, 1993), some gifted learners develop problems when their educational needs are not met or when their socio-emotional needs are not recognized and addressed.

Rationale

Children who are gifted are extremely varied and typically have a wide range of guidance needs. Many young gifted learners are confused when their age peers do not learn as quickly as they do or when teachers do not provide adequately challenging learning activities (Kerr, 1991). Young gifted learners often display uneven development (Roedell, 1989; Silverman, 1993), as when a 6-year-old has academic skills at the fourth-grade level, but both motor and social skills typical of his or her age. Some gifted learners frustrate parents and teachers when they display unusual levels of independence at early ages (Maxwell, 1998). Other gifted learners are far more intense than average children (Piechowski, 1997). Both gifted boys (Alvino, 1991) and gifted girls (Reis, 1991) may need assistance, especially if their choices for social activity, education, or careers are considered unsuitable for their gender.

Benefits

1. Gifted learners whose social and emotional needs are addressed are more likely to be able to focus on their academic needs.

Potential Barriers

1. Undesirable behaviors or emotional intensity exhibited by gifted learners may be interpreted as disobedient or problematic.
2. Efforts might be made to "correct" problems or issues with the child when it may be the environment that needs to be addressed.
3. Counselors may not be available at all levels, pre-K–12, to serve the life planning and socio-emotional needs of any students, much less gifted learners.
4. Most counselors are generally not trained to meet the unique needs of gifted learners.
5. Gifted learners may be challenging to the counselor given advanced critical analysis processes.

Standards and Sample Outcomes

|

Gifted learners, because of their unique socio-emotional development, must be provided with guidance and counseling services by a counselor who is familiar with the characteristics and socio-emotional needs of gifted learners.

- Counselors are trained to help gifted learners through problems of perfectionism, isolation, and other vulnerabilities, individually or in small groups.
- Upon receiving initial gifted education programming services, gifted learners are made aware of counseling and guidance services and the match to the students' specific needs.
- Educators and parents are aware of the uneven development typical of gifted learners.

Counseling services should be provided by a counselor familiar with specific training in the characteristics and socio-emotional needs (e.g., underachievement, multipotentiality, etc.) of diverse gifted learners.

- The counselor assigned to work with gifted learners has formal training in working with this population of students.
- The counselor is able to work effectively with parents and teachers in better understanding and addressing the socio-emotional needs of gifted students.

Gifted learners must be provided with career guidance services especially designed for their unique needs.

Description

Gifted learners need to learn about many potential careers beginning at an earlier age than most students. For example, gifted girls often do not realize the necessity of taking challenging math courses to help them prepare for science and math-oriented careers (Kerr, 1991).

Rationale

Gifted learners have career guidance or life-planning needs unlike those of their peers. For example, gifted learners have been reported to have difficulty making choices among all the career possibilities available to them because, as a group, they have multiple skills and multiple interests (Kerr, 1991). However, recent research has demonstrated that the use of above-level traditional assessment tools combined with individually focused feedback may help gifted learners to identify relative strengths and weaknesses, as well as help them to understand their abilities and preferences more effectively than has been previously understood (Achter, Benbow, & Lubinski, 1997).

Benefits

1. Gifted learners who are assisted in making appropriate choices about career pathways are less likely to waste valuable time trying to make decisions given their multipotentiality.
2. Gifted learners can pursue more career options when appropriately advised, such as enrolling in as many advanced math and science courses as possible to be in a better position to pursue a broader variety of career options.

Potential Barriers

1. Family and the community may discourage gifted learners of either gender if they are perceived to be interested in careers dominated by the opposite gender.
2. Parents may oppose counseling efforts that encourage students to consider a wide range of careers, including those that the parents may not support.

Standards and Sample Outcomes

Gifted learners must be provided with career guidance consistent with their unique strengths.

- Counseling strategies are implemented that address the multipotentiality of gifted learners.
- Beginning in the primary grades, gifted learners are introduced to varying professions and occupations as desirable to both genders.
- For gifted girls, in particular, the guidance counselor encourages extensive enrollment in courses in science and math beginning in the middle grades.

Gifted learners should be provided with college and career guidance that is appropriately different and delivered earlier than typical programs.

- As part of career guidance, gifted learners have the opportunity to meet professionals in the fields that appeal to them and to "shadow" them on the job.
- Gifted learners have opportunities to observe professionals in areas matching potential and interests, rather than stereotypes of gender, socio-economic status, race, or ethnicity.
- If location permits, high schools consider partnerships with a college or university for sharing career guidance opportunities to gifted learners.
- Schools offer mentor experiences to gifted learners in order to encourage student contact with professionals from a variety of fields.

Gifted at-risk students must be provided with guidance and counseling to help them reach their potential.

Description

Students who are at risk are more likely to experience barriers to academic progress and may need assistance to reach their full potential.

Rationale

Stereotyped expectations and other factors separate from intellectual ability may keep gifted learners from at-risk populations from being recognized as gifted by the schools or from doing well academically. Such students may include gifted learners with disabilities (Johnson, Karnes, & Carr, 1997), disadvantaged gifted learners (Olszewski-Kubilius & Scott, 1992), and students from cultural minorities (Bands, 1989; Ford, 1996). Even when they do well in elementary and secondary schools, their families may not have sufficient knowledge of the system to help them in the college selection and application process. A lack of awareness of their financial needs or of the financial assistance system may further penalize them (Olszewski-Kubilius & Scott). Gifted females in particular may have issues that inhibit them from reaching their potential or from deriving satisfaction from their accomplishments.

Benefits

1. Gifted learners who come from at-risk populations have much to gain when they are recognized and their academic needs are appropriately addressed.
2. Society benefits when all gifted learners are successful in school and then move into careers where their talents help them to make significant contributions.
3. Greater achievement by gifted learners from at-risk populations can also help to improve society's perception of groups believed to be less capable.

Potential Barriers

1. Parents may, directly or indirectly, communicate to their children that higher education is neither desirable nor necessary (McIntosh & Greenlaw, 1986). Other parents may create stress to attend particular colleges that are not appropriate given the student's career goals.
2. Parents who lack experience with the college application process may not be able to assist their children adequately.
3. African American gifted learners may be torn between cultural expectations and the expectations of their peers and staff involved in gifted education programming if they perceive them to be incompatible (Ford, 1996).

Standards and Sample Outcomes

Gifted learners who are at risk must have special attention, counseling, and support to help them realize their full potential.

- Specialized programs for advanced studies and career development are provided to economically disadvantaged gifted learners.
- Gifted learners from at-risk populations who are not performing well academically because of factors other than intellectual ability receive assistance to strengthen those areas that prevent them from performing at higher levels.
- Gifted learners are provided assistance in the college selection and application processes, including the procedures for locating and applying for financial aid.

Gifted learners who do not demonstrate satisfactory performance in regular and/or gifted education classes should be provided with specialized intervention services.

- Gifted learners who have difficulty with standardized test formats are provided instruction in test-taking skills.
- Teachers and counselors working with at-risk gifted learners address the learners' strengths and weaknesses and differentiate strategies according to their diverse needs.

Gifted learners must be provided with affective curriculum in addition to differentiated guidance and counseling services.

Description

High-ability students need specific curriculum that addresses their socio-emotional needs and enhances development of the whole child, rather than just their cognitive development.

Rationale

Although gifted learners often realize that they are different from their same age peers, they rarely have opportunities to discuss their giftedness and its impact on their lives (Colangelo, 1997). Gifted learners with advanced abilities, such as a higher degree of perceptiveness than age peers, may interpret this difference negatively unless they have assistance in accepting such strengths (Delisle, 1992). Gifted students often need help learning to take reasonable risks in areas outside their comfort levels, but they can learn how to do this productively (Neihart, 1999). Gifted learners may suffer because they have few intellectual peers, except for students in higher grades (Delisle).

Benefits

1. Given appropriate direction, gifted learners can learn to take appropriate risks and can learn to appreciate their abilities without seeing themselves as "better than" their age peers.
2. Gifted learners who are comfortable with their abilities are more likely to use their talents in positive ways.

Potential Barriers

1. School counseling staffs are unlikely to have had specific training in guiding and counseling gifted learners.

Standards and Sample Outcomes

4.0 Minimum Standard	4.0 Exemplary Standard
Gifted learners must be provided with affective curriculum as part of differentiated curriculum and instructional services.	*A well-defined and implemented affective curriculum scope and sequence containing personal/social awareness and adjustment, academic planning, and vocational and career awareness should be provided to gifted learners.*

- Counseling is offered that specifically helps gifted learners in understanding and accepting their particular developmental differences.
- Upon initial involvement in gifted education programming, gifted learners participate in activities designed to help them understand themselves as gifted persons.
- Gifted learners are taught how to advocate for themselves and solve some of their own academic and socio-emotional problems.

- An affective curriculum with appropriate scope and sequence is developed so that, at every level of gifted education programming, affective needs of the appropriate developmental period can be addressed for those needing such opportunities.
- A trained counselor provides opportunities for students to participate in regular group discussion around issues related to giftedness (especially for adolescent students and gifted girls).
- Gifted learners are provided assistance in understanding and respecting individual differences in positive ways.

Underachieving gifted learners must be served, rather than omitted from differentiated services.

Description

Gifted learners who are performing at a significantly lower level than expected are unlikely to improve on their own, but should be helped toward better performance by teachers and counselors.

Rationale

Regardless of the reasons why gifted learners underachieve, most such students have low self-concepts and view themselves negatively (Kerr, 1991). Removing such students from special educational programming because of low performance may simply reinforce their negative views of themselves without improving student performance. In some cases, moving the student to a more challenging academic placement is sufficient for correcting the problem. For other students, such moves must be accompanied by counseling strategies.

Benefits

1. Helping nonachieving gifted learners attain expected achievement levels contributes to a positive sense of self-efficacy and more positive adjustment.

Potential Barriers

1. Teachers and parents who become convinced that the student is intentionally performing poorly are often not receptive to examining their own roles in the situation. School districts may adopt a punitive position and establish rules that automatically remove students from programming when performance drops below the expected level.

Standards and Sample Outcomes

Gifted students who are underachieving must not be exited from gifted programs because of related problems.

- Counselors and teachers advocate for a school policy that allows underachieving gifted learners to be retained, rather than removed from gifted education programming.
- Counselors and teachers meet routinely with parents of gifted learners to develop good rapport so that they can work together more effectively if a student's achievement drops.

Underachieving gifted learners should be provided with specific guidance and counseling services that address the issues and problems related to underachievement.

- Counselors and teachers involved in gifted education programming are routinely provided in-service training to help them understand that the complexity of most underachievement problems requires attention for the student, not the punishment of being removed from services.
- Counselors develop collaborative plans for working with underachieving gifted learners that involve parents and teachers, as well as the students.

4 Student Identification

by Susan J. Hansford, Ph.D., Aimee M. Bonar, Jeanine M. Scally, and Nicole A. Burge

Gifted learners must be assessed to determine appropriate educational services.

Student assessment for gifted identification is an organized, systematic, ongoing process that seeks to identify student needs for purposes of matching students to programming options. General principles for identification of gifted students were identified by Callahan and McIntire (1994): (1) using assessments that go beyond a narrowed conception of talent; (2) using separate and appropriate identification strategies to identify different aspects of giftedness; (3) using reliable and valid instruments and strategies for assessing the construct of talent underlying the definition; (4) using appropriate instruments with underserved populations; (5) viewing each child as an individual and recognizing the limits of a single score on any measure; (6) using a multiple-measure/multiple-criteria approach to identification; (7) recognizing the serious limitations of using matrices in the identification process and appreciating the value of the individual case study; and (8) identifying and placing students based on student need and ability, rather than on numbers that can be served by a program.

A comprehensive and cohesive process for student nomination must be coordinated in order to determine eligibility for gifted education services.

Description

The exclusive use of standardized tests and other objective measures is not sufficient for appropriate student identification. Multiple sources of information about students provide a more accurate assessment of abilities and needs. Nomination of students for gifted education services provides important information about students' abilities. Strategies and procedures that promote involvement of all school staff, as well as students, families, and community members, support student access to the gifted identification process and subsequent services.

Rationale

A comprehensive process for student nomination helps to avoid eliminating potentially gifted students from consideration for services. The use of nominations from a variety of sources in the identification process can provide information about students' abilities that traditional testing procedures may overlook. Parents provide important information about their child's development and behaviors in a nonschool setting. Nominations by teachers and other school personnel are most useful when those individuals have received some training in the nature of giftedness and when they are provided with specific behaviors or characteristics on which to base nomination (Borland, 1989). In addition to referrals from adults, research has shown that not only do students express the desire to nominate themselves and other students, but that there do not appear to be detrimental effects in doing so (Masse & Gagné, 1996). Peer nominations have specific benefits in that students have opportunities to observe behavior that does not occur in the classroom setting (Masse & Gagné). A cohesive nomination process ensures that nominations obtained from a variety of sources are based on common understandings about giftedness and student characteristics. Coordinated nomination processes encourage and support rather than inhibit and discourage nomination.

Benefits

1. A comprehensive, cohesive, and coordinated process for student nomination results in more accurate and equitable identification of gifted students.
2. The use of multiple sources of information can yield important information about students' abilities that can be overlooked using only objective data.
3. Comprehensive nomination processes can allow opportunity for consideration of potentially gifted students who might otherwise be screened out of further assessment or consideration for services.
4. Participation in nomination processes may lead to better understanding and sensitivity to the needs of gifted students.
5. A comprehensive nomination process provides opportunities for finding atypical student referrals from unlikely sources. For example, the nomination of students with dual exceptionalities from special education teachers.

Potential Barriers

1. Misperceptions and misunderstandings regarding giftedness, characteristics of gifted students, and the need for educational services for gifted students may limit the effectiveness of nomination procedures.

2. Sufficient resources (time, money, personnel) must be allocated for wide distribution of information, for responding to concerns, and for correcting misperceptions.

Standards and Sample Outcomes

1.0 Minimum Standard

Information regarding the characteristics of gifted students in areas served by the district must be annually disseminated to all appropriate staff members.

- All appropriate staff members (i.e., teachers, counselors, administrators) annually receive information regarding student nomination procedures, characteristics of gifted students, and gifted education services. Information regarding the characteristics and behaviors associated with giftedness includes specific examples that will enable informed nominations.
- Staff who work in the visual and performing arts receive information annually regarding giftedness in this domain.
- Staff who work in specialized programming service areas, such as special education, should be provided information about gifted learners they might encounter, such as students with dual exceptionalities.
- Dissemination strategies include staff development activities, as well as written materials.

1.0 Exemplary Standard

The school district should provide information annually, in a variety of languages, regarding the process for nominating students for gifted education programming services.

- Information about student nomination procedures, characteristics of gifted students, and gifted education services is provided annually to a wide audience, including families, community members, students, and all school staff.
- This information is available to families and the community in the languages in which they are most fluent and through modes of communication readily available to the audience (e.g., brochures, take-home materials, web site information, library access).
- Information is provided to other instructors in the community, such as dance and music teachers, and provided without educational jargon.

1.1 Minimum Standard

All students must comprise the initial screening pool of potential recipients of gifted education services.

- Nominations are solicited in such a way as to facilitate access for all students.
- Students are not excluded from potential nomination because of test scores, school performance, or other criteria.
- The pool for gifted learners in the visual and performing arts extends beyond students enrolled in courses in this area.
- Special populations of gifted learners are screened, such as students with dual exceptionalities or students who are underachieving.

1.1 Exemplary Standard

The nomination process should be ongoing, and screening of any student should occur at any time.

- The pool of students who may be nominated includes all students.
- Once nominated, students are screened within a reasonable time period, rather than waiting for a specified, scheduled time within the school year.
- Because emerging talent in the visual and performing arts is related to developmental levels and ages, the nomination process in this area must be open.

Standards and Sample Outcomes continued

Nominations for services must be accepted from any source (e.g., teachers, parents, community members, peers, etc.).

- Specific procedures are in place for soliciting and accepting nominations for services from multiple sources.
- Information about nomination procedures is widely distributed and easily accessible to nonschool as well as school sources.
- Nominations for students in the visual and performing arts are solicited from community resources, such as after-school programs, private instructors, schools of dance, music, and art, and so forth.

Nomination procedures and forms should be available in a variety of languages.

- All written materials regarding nomination (i.e., procedures, forms, characteristics information) are available in the language in which the parent, student, or community member is most fluent and through modes of communication that are readily accessible by the audience.
- Informational meetings, workshops, or seminars for parents about the nomination process involve interpreters as necessary or are transcribed into the appropriate languages.
- Information regarding nomination procedures must be presented to community instructors in a format and language appropriate to their professions.

Parents must be provided with information regarding an understanding of giftedness and student characteristics.

- Nomination forms include information about giftedness and characteristics of gifted students.
- Additional information about giftedness and characteristics of gifted students is available to parents upon request.
- School libraries contain materials specifically for parents related to giftedness.

Parents should be provided with special workshops or seminars to get a full meaning of giftedness.

- Informational meetings, workshops, or seminars about the nature of giftedness are open to all parents.
- Comprehensive examples are provided of how giftedness may manifest itself differently in various cultures and in nonschool settings.
- Training opportunities occur throughout the school year and in a variety of settings to encourage attendance and participation.

Instruments used for student assessment to determine eligibility for gifted education services must measure diverse abilities, talents, strengths, and needs in order to provide students an opportunity to demonstrate any strengths.

Description

Data collection strategies should ensure that instructional planners are provided with information that will guide placement decisions. The data should also provide information for teachers to use in making subsequent instructional decisions. These data should reflect expanded conceptions of intelligence.

Rationale

Increased understandings about intelligence have led to broader definitions of giftedness. However, there still exists an over-reliance in the identification process on instruments that measure narrow conceptions of giftedness (Maker, 1996). Certain populations of children—especially those from racial, cultural, and ethnic minority populations, from low-SES environments, and those with disabilities or for whom English is a second language—are often overlooked in the gifted identification process. Issues of bias (racial, ethnic, economic, gender, or age) may limit nominations of potentially gifted students. Issues affecting the technical adequacy of instruments can result in bias against certain populations of gifted students (Ford, 1998); therefore, a full range of procedures and instruments must be considered. Further, assessments of general aptitude provide only limited information for appropriate adaptations of instruction.

Benefits

1. The use of assessment instruments and procedures that provide multiple opportunities to demonstrate strengths can result in more equitable identification and resulting access to services for children who previously were overlooked.
2. Data that provide specific information on student strengths and weaknesses, accomplishments, and prior responses to instruction will make instruction more effective and efficient.

Potential Barriers

1. The lack of appropriate assessment instruments, limitations and technical adequacy of assessment instruments, and possible bias in assessment instruments can limit the ability to measure diverse abilities, talents, strengths, and needs.
2. State identification requirements may put restrictions on the areas of giftedness that may be assessed, the assessment instruments and procedures that may be used, and/or the criteria that must be met to receive services.

Standards and Sample Outcomes

2.0 Minimum Standard

Assessment instruments must measure the capabilities of students with provisions for the language in which the student is most fluent, when available.

- The selection and use of assessment instruments take into consideration the language in which the student is most fluent.
- Assessment instruments and procedures available in a child's native language are used when available and appropriate. An interpreter is used if the administrator for the assessment is not fluent in the child's language.

2.0 Exemplary Standard

Assessments should be provided in a language in which the student is most fluent, if available.

- Prior to formal assessment, test administrators assess second-language learners to determine the language in which the child is most fluent and then administer assessments in the appropriate language.
- Alternative assessment or performance-based assessment procedures conducted in the visual and performing arts are conducted in the language in which the student is most fluent or includes provisions for translation.

2.1 Minimum Standard

Assessments must be culturally fair.

- Assessment instruments were normed on diverse populations from a variety of geographical locations.
- Assessment instruments and strategies conform to professional standards of practice.
- Alternative assessments used for measuring intellectual and academic aptitudes, as well as performances used in the visual and performing arts are consistent with the expression of giftedness indicative of a given culture.

2.1 Exemplary Standard

Assessment should be responsive to students' economic conditions, gender, developmental differences, handicapping conditions, and other factors that mitigate against fair assessment practices.

- Assessment instruments and strategies conform to professional standards of practice.
- The appropriateness of assessment instruments and strategies for different populations of students is evaluated prior to their selection. Strategies and instruments are selected that are not biased for or against any given population of students.
- Assessment procedures are consistent with the developmental nature of talent for any individual gifted learner.

2.2 Minimum Standard

The purpose(s) of student assessments must be consistently articulated across all grade levels.

- Assessments are conducted to identify targeted student needs and to align those needs with optimal student placement in available services.
- The purpose of assessments conducted at one grade level is consistent with developmental needs and subsequent educational decision making at all other grade levels.
- Assessment approaches for identifying gifted learners in the visual and performing arts are consistent with the development stage of specific children at each grade level.
- Policies, written documentation, and informational meetings exist to articulate the purpose of assessment at various grade levels.

2.2 Exemplary Standard

Students identified in all designated areas of giftedness within a school district should be assessed consistently across grade levels.

- A systematic process is in place to ensure consideration for appropriate assessment of students in all grade levels in all designated areas of giftedness.
- Assessment procedures across all grade levels and areas of giftedness meet the same high standards of professional practice.
- Students are reassessed as appropriate to assure that differentiated services are aligned with the students' educational and developmental needs.
- The assessment of students' aptitudes in the visual and performing arts is sensitive to emerging talent issues.

2.3 Minimum Standard

Student assessments must be sensitive to the current stage of talent development.

- Assessment instruments are not limited by low ceilings of performance and norms that are not appropriate for the developmental level of the student.
- Assessments of achievement in visual and performing arts are sensitive to the lack of nurturing of these nonacademic aptitudes.

2.3 Exemplary Standard

Student assessments should be sensitive to all stages of talent development.

- Assessment instruments and strategies take into consideration that talent development may not be fully realized, therefore, remaining as emerging, rather than actualized talent.
- Assessment instruments and procedures acknowledge the difference between potential and current performance.

A student assessment profile of individual strengths and needs must be developed to plan appropriate intervention.

Description

The assessment paradigm for the identification of giftedness must reflect a comprehensive view of each child, such as that presented by a profile of the student, rather than the more limited view presented by a single score on any measure (Callahan & McIntire, 1994). Therefore, a profile portrays the strengths and weaknesses of a child in a manner that provides data for sound instructional planning.

Rationale

The process of screening for and identifying giftedness is not effective and efficient unless services are related to assessment (Mendaglio & Pyryt, 1995). Data collected through the assessment process must guide subsequent changes in curriculum and instruction.

Benefits

1. Information obtained through appropriate screening and identification processes can inform educational decision making and enable a closer alignment of educational needs to services.

Potential Barriers

1. The construction and use of appropriate individual profiles for students requires collection of a variety of data, careful record keeping, and the ability to analyze and synthesize data.
2. Sufficient resources must be allocated to accomplish the collection, collation, and analysis of data for individual students.

Standards and Sample Outcomes

3.0 Minimum Standard

An assessment profile must be developed for each child to evaluate eligibility for gifted education programming services.

- Student placement is based on needs demonstrated by a profile of strengths and weaknesses, not on the number of program "slots" available.
- Districts do not use a matrix process in which scores from assessment strategies and instruments that measure different constructs are added together.
- Portfolios used to collect data for gifted learners in the academic arena and in the visual and performing arts must provide a comprehensive assessment of giftedness.

3.0 Exemplary Standard

Individual assessment plans should be developed for all gifted learners who need gifted education.

- A variety of assessment procedures and instruments, based on individual differences and needs, are readily available.
- Eligibility for services is based on a comprehensive analysis of student needs, rather than on one score or on only one type of assessment method.
- Individual case studies are developed for students in both academics and visual and performing arts.

3.1 Minimum Standard

An assessment profile must reflect the unique learning characteristics and potential and performance levels.

- The assessment profile provides information about the learning characteristics of gifted students, as well as projected and current functioning.

3.1 Exemplary Standard

An assessment profile should reflect the gifted learner's interests, learning style, and educational needs.

- The assessment profile reflects the uniqueness of the individual gifted student.
- The assessment instruments and procedures provide information relative to determining the specific needs of individual students.

All student identification procedures and instruments must be based on current theory and research.

Description

Identification procedures and instruments should be investigated through a review of current literature, which includes test reviews prior to use to determine their appropriateness for the construct being assessed and for the district's population of students. The use of assessment instruments should conform to professional standards for ethical use, as well as reflect current best practice and research for the specific use with gifted learners.

Rationale

The research literature from the fields of gifted child education and psychology provides information about identification procedures and instruments that is continually changing. If the most current information is not applied, students might be missed as a result of out-of-date instrumentation or procedure. As new information and insights are reported, expanded conceptions of giftedness and talent and expanded understandings about the reliability and validity of assessment instruments require a realignment of definitions and methods used for assessment and identification (Maker, 1996; Rogers, 1998).

Benefits

1. Use of current theory and research to aid decision making about student identification procedures and instruments ensures that district procedures are appropriate for their students.
2. Current research includes new or modified procedure and instrumentation that may improve the likelihood that traditionally overlooked gifted learners will be appropriately assessed for giftedness.

Potential Barriers

1. Access to current theory and research may be difficult for some districts.
2. An emphasis on quick decisions, ease of identification practices, and basing decisions solely on pragmatics can inhibit thorough investigation and analysis of identification strategies.

Standards and Sample Outcomes

4.0 Minimum Standard

No single assessment instrument or its results denies student eligibility for gifted programming services.

- A battery of assessment instruments and procedures provide more than one "path" to eligibility so that results from one instrument do not automatically exclude a student who warrants a closer examination.
- Student performance or demonstration of visual and performing arts ability is representative of work over time, rather than a one-time display of aptitude.

4.0 Exemplary Standard

Student assessment data should come from multiple sources and include multiple assessment methods.

- Districts use a balanced combination of strategies that permit multiple ways for potentially gifted children to be identified. Placement decisions also are based on multiple sources of information.
- Assessments of visual and performing arts incorporate a diverse display of talent collected by several approaches.

4.1 Minimum Standard

All assessment instruments must provide evidence of reliability and validity for the intended purposes and target students.

- Assessment instruments and procedures are selected based on satisfactory reliability and validity for their intended use in identifying giftedness.
- In evaluating the technical adequacy of any assessment method or instrument, districts use data from research studies about the method or instrument in addition to the data provided by the author and/or publisher.
- When assessment instruments are renormed or outdated, their use is revisited.
- At the very least, interrater reliability is established among experts who assess performances and displays of work in assessing visual and performing arts talent.

4.1 Exemplary Standard

Student assessment data should represent an appropriate balance of reliable and valid quantitative and qualitative measures.

- Sources of student assessment data are balanced between academic and nonacademic sources, formal and informal strategies, standardized and nonstandardized assessments, subjective and objective data, and qualitative and quantitative data.
- Districts document the reliability and validity of each assessment instrument and procedure for the purposes of identifying gifted students in their school setting.

Written procedures for student identification must include, at the very least, provisions for informed consent, student retention, student reassessment, student exiting, and appeals procedures.

Description

Clearly articulated procedures must guide student identification and placement practices. All procedures should seek to protect the rights of students. Specific steps and criteria for screening, assessment, and decisions related to placement, as well as procedures for informed consent and a process for appeal are included. All procedures should be in written form and provided to parents and other stakeholders.

Rationale

Although special education students have been entitled to due process through federal legislation for the past quarter-century, gifted students have not been afforded the same protection in all states. In the absence of such legislation, schools have not always been as diligent as they might be in their approach to identifying and serving gifted students, resulting in issues related to access to services and denial of due process.

Benefits

1. The articulation of specific procedures for student identification, placement decisions, informed consent, and appeals can result in more equitable and appropriate identification and placement of students.
2. Providing those procedures in written form to all stakeholders, including parents, can support the educational decision-making process.

Potential Barriers

1. In some schools, the large number of foreign languages spoken by families in the district make the written documentation of all identification procedures burdensome.

Standards and Sample Outcomes

5.0 Minimum Standard

District gifted programming guidelines must contain specific procedures for student assessment at least once during the elementary, middle, and secondary levels.

- Assessment of students is consistent with different developmental stages to gauge current needs.
- Assessment occurs at least once at the elementary, middle, and secondary levels so that no gifted learner is missed or dismissed by a one-time-only identification procedure.

5.0 Exemplary Standard

Student placement data should be collected using an appropriate balance of quantitative and qualitative measures with adequate evidence of reliability and validity for the purposes of identification.

- Student placement involves the collection of information related to the students' needs.
- Student placement is based on a balance of varied measures that provide reliable and valid evidence for the identification of educational needs.
- The data collected during the student assessment and placement process are recorded in written records for each screened or assessed student.
- Assessment and placement process records are maintained by the school and provided to the parent upon request.

5.1 Minimum Standard

District guidelines must provide specific procedures for student retention and exiting, as well as guidelines for parent appeals.

- Specific criteria are used for placement in services, retention in services, and exiting or withdrawal from services.
- These criteria promote entitlement for services, rather than privilege, and reflect an emphasis on aligning services with assessed needs.
- Parents who do not agree with assessment results, recommended educational services, or changes in placement may appeal those decisions by following clearly articulated district guidelines.

5.1 Exemplary Standard

District guidelines and procedures should be reviewed and revised when necessary.

- Districts conduct an evaluation of student identification and placement procedures on a regular basis.
- All aspects of the procedures are evaluated: adequacy of the procedures, implementation of the procedures, and effectiveness of the procedures.
- Results of the evaluation are documented in written form.
- Data obtained from the evaluation are used to revise procedures as indicated.
- Revisions to procedures reflect the most current practice and empirical findings available.

5 Curriculum and Instruction

by Kimberley Chandler

> Gifted education services must include curricular and instructional opportunities directed to the unique needs of the gifted learner.

Gifted education services must include curricular and instructional opportunities directed to the specific needs of gifted learners. "No area of emphasis within gifted education better captures its core concepts than does the area of curriculum" (VanTassel–Baska, 1998, p. 339). The critical role of curriculum in shaping the talent development process must be understood and supported by practitioners so that the school environment is responsive. According to Maker (1982), the appropriate school curriculum for gifted children is "qualitatively different from the program for nongifted students" (p. 3).

Differentiated curriculum for the gifted learner must span grades pre-K–12.

Description

The particular needs of gifted learners may be addressed at all levels of schooling through the implementation of a differentiated curriculum. Differentiation may involve modification of content, process, product, and/or learning environment (Tomlinson, 1999).

Rationale

Gifted children have specific behavioral characteristics in the cognitive and affective realms that present special learning needs that must be addressed by curriculum differentiation (VanTassel-Baska, 1998). Differentiation provides a means of addressing the particular characteristics and promoting the continual growth of students in an environment that is respectful of individual differences (Tomlinson, 1999).

Benefits

1. Continual progress for gifted learners is promoted when differentiated curricula and instruction span all grade levels.
2. Gifted learners' entry and exit points in the general curriculum are different at all levels of development; therefore, curriculum differentiation provides for necessary modifications at all grade levels.
3. Early mastery of content and skills and continuous progress lead to sustained advanced learning rates across all grade levels.

Potential Barriers

1. There are varying definitions of the term *differentiation*.
2. At the classroom level, problematic issues include the teachers' lack of content knowledge, teachers' lack of special methods training, and the wide spectrum of student abilities (Gallagher, 1985).

Standards and Sample Outcomes

1.0 Minimum Standard	1.0 Exemplary Standard

Differentiated curriculum (curricular and instructional adaptations that address the unique learning needs of gifted learners) for gifted learners must be integrated and articulated throughout the district.

A well-defined and implemented curriculum scope and sequence should be articulated for all grade levels and all subject areas.

- School and district leadership must support differentiation through modification of policies and procedures related to curriculum.
- Differentiated curriculum is developed at the district level, rather than at the instructional unit or school level.
- Differentiated curriculum is implemented in core academic areas, creativity, leadership, and the visual and performing arts.

- Curriculum scope and sequence articulates how curriculum differentiation at each grade level within given subject areas is based on connections between previous and subsequent learning experiences.
- The relationship of specialized programs of study, such as art and music, to differentiated programming in the visual and performing arts is clearly articulated.

Regular classroom curricula and instruction must be adapted, modified, or replaced to meet the unique needs of gifted learners.

Description

The level of curricular materials and the related instructional methods are crucial for meeting the needs of gifted learners. "The emphasis in the special programs for gifted learners is on the stimulation of the thinking processes of creativity, originality, problem solving, and of increasing the content depth and sophistication" (Gallagher, 1985, p. 82). While these elements should certainly be present in programming for all children, the difference for gifted learners is related to the need for a greater depth, complexity, and so forth.

Rationale

In a statement of support for curriculum compacting, Reis, Burns, and Renzulli (1992) delineated some of the problematic issues facing gifted students in the regular classroom: (1) low conceptual level of textbooks; (2) students' knowledge of textbook content and the resulting repetition of content; and (3) failure of teachers to meet the needs of high-ability students. From an analysis of recommended program practices for gifted learners, Shore and Delcourt (1996) determined that the use of high-level curricular materials was one of five practices that received strong support in the research as a practice uniquely appropriate to gifted education. VanTassel–Baska (1994) advocated an approach that combines linkage to world-class standards and recognition of a developmental perspective on fostering student abilities.

Benefits

1. Curriculum and instruction modification and adaptation must occur in order for gifted learners to realize their full potential.
2. Curricular and instructional modifications may reduce boredom from redundancy for gifted learners.
3. Another beneficiary of the special modifications for gifted learners includes teachers, in terms of their professional growth, as they develop the skills and methodologies for working with gifted learners.
4. Teachers who modify and adapt curricula and instruction will assess student progress in order to establish new learning goals.

Potential Barriers

1. The need for teacher training, money, and time are barriers to the development and use of appropriate curricula and instruction for gifted learners.
2. Emphasis on equity can lead to opposition to specialized services offered for some, but not all students. This may lead to a gradual decrease of monies budgeted for gifted programs or to the eventual termination of services.

Standards and Sample Outcomes

2.0 Minimum Standard

Instruction, objectives, and strategies provided gifted learners must be systematically differentiated from those in the regular classroom.

- Individuals involved in gifted education programming obtain training and experience related to the elements of differentiation.
- Differentiation of classroom learning applies to all subject matter and content areas, including the visual and performing arts and technical arts.
- A diagnostic-prescriptive approach to educational planning allows for a determination of the degree to which teaching and learning activities should be differentiated appropriately for any given learner.

2.0 Exemplary Standard

District curriculum plans should include objectives, content, and resources that challenge gifted learners in the regular classroom.

- The instructional component outlines the curriculum model(s) on which the program is built, as well as the content, process, and product emphases; curricular objectives; and resources.
- District curriculum plans for gifted education programming are written to provide a sense of direction and purpose. The plan provides an essential communication about what is distinctive about the curriculum in terms of its appropriateness for gifted learners.
- Educational planning includes all subject areas, as well as the technical and visual and performing arts.

2.1 Minimum Standard

Teachers must differentiate, replace, supplement, or modify curricula to facilitate higher level learning goals.

- Qualitative changes made to facilitate higher level learning goals include curriculum compacting and the subsequent modification of content, process, product, and learning environment.
- Differentiation occurs in place of, rather than in addition to, grade-level expectations.

2.1 Exemplary Standard

Teachers should be responsible for developing plans to differentiate the curriculum in every discipline for gifted learners.

- Clearly articulated curriculum goals and objectives are the framework for differentiating instruction for gifted learners.
- Planning for district-wide differentiation is guided by a framework with a suggested scope and sequence and unit plans.
- Teachers make modifications based on student strengths, interests, abilities, and achievement levels, as well as their learning styles.
- Entry and exit points in the curriculum are established for students at regular intervals.

Standards and Sample Outcomes continued

Means for demonstrating proficiency in essential regular curriculum concepts and processes must be established to facilitate appropriate academic acceleration.

- Acceleration includes options such as grade skipping, subject skipping, early admission, or dual enrollment programs.
- School districts articulate the options available and the means through which students will be screened for participation in such options.
- A district protocol must be established to address the processes through which acceleration will occur.
- Diagnostic testing, performance-based assessments, and observation of mastery are techniques employed for demonstrating proficiency and essential skills.
- Guidelines for facilitating appropriate acceleration should include a consideration of demonstrated academic ability, an appraisal of the student's intellectual and social adjustment, family dynamics, and the school district's capacity to support the child.

Documentation of instruction for assessing level(s) of learning and accelerated rates of learning should demonstrate plans for gifted learners based on specific needs of individual learners.

- A diagnostic-prescriptive approach may be utilized for modification of core curricular content for the individual learner.
- Appropriate entry and exit points in the curriculum and accelerated paces of learning are accommodated for gifted learning in all disciplines, both academic and nonacademic.

2.3 Minimum Standard	2.3 Exemplary Standard

Gifted learners must be assessed for proficiency in basic skills and knowledge and provided with alternative challenging educational opportunities when proficiency is demonstrated.

Gifted learners should be assessed for proficiency in all standard courses of study and subsequently provided with educational opportunities that are more challenging.

- Flexibility regarding issues of student learning is essential for meeting the needs of gifted learners.
- A menu of programming options is available when competence is demonstrated in basic skill areas.
- Gifted learners are allowed to make continuous progress by testing out of previously mastered material.

- A protocol for assessing student proficiency in all standard courses of study is used to determine placement in optional services.
- The individual student's demonstration of ability, readiness, and motivation is considered before placement in optional opportunities is made.
- Both grouping practices and acceleration may be employed as approaches to serving students who have demonstrated proficiency in standard courses of study.

Instructional pace must be flexible to allow for the accelerated learning of gifted learners as appropriate.

Description

Pace refers to the rate or tempo of instruction. For gifted learners, activities must move at a rate that is comfortable and matches their mental processing speed. The instructional pace must be flexible so that the learners are challenged, but also so that they are given time to think about ideas and process information.

Rationale

Gifted students learn at different speeds, and they differ in ability to think at advanced levels (Tomlinson, 1999). Varying the instructional pace is an important strategy for delivering curricula appropriately to the gifted learner. The differentiation of learning pace merely offers several avenues for learning to gifted learners (Tomlinson). Appropriate pacing often relates to providing a brief review of material already learned or to summarizing key concepts at the beginning of a lesson (VanTassel-Baska, 1992), then allowing students to learn at their own rate.

Benefits

1. When the instructional pace is flexible, accelerated, in-depth learning may occur because less time is spent on basic skills and concepts.
2. Flexible instructional pacing allows for an optimal match between instructional purposes, curriculum, setting, and student needs.

Potential Barriers

1. Classroom management is often an obstacle to implementation.
2. Some districts practice instructional or management strategies that restrict the movement of students through the curriculum at different rates.
3. Parental anxiety regarding students' reluctance to let students move ahead faster or farther than their same-age peers may present a barrier to flexible pacing practices.

Standards and Sample Outcomes

3.0 Minimum Standard	3.0 Exemplary Standard

A program of instruction must consist of advanced content and appropriately differentiated teaching strategies to reflect the accelerative learning pace and advanced intellectual processes of gifted learners.

- Administrative arrangements that enhance or restrict the quality of the instructional setting for the gifted learner are considered when selecting teaching strategies.
- Advanced content is taught through differentiated instructional strategies that are deemed most appropriate for meeting the needs of gifted learners.
- Varied rates of instruction are accompanied with varied degrees of complexity of content.

When warranted, continual opportunities for curricular acceleration should be provided in gifted learners' areas of strength and interest while allowing sufficient ceiling for optimal learning.

- Assess the most appropriate entrance and exit points in the curriculum for gifted learners, including independent study, early entrance, early exit, dual enrollment, and advanced placement.
- Age should not be a sole determinant of instructional pace for any gifted learner.
- Differentiated learning experiences are sensitive to individual differences in pacing, approaches to learning, and modes of student expression (Tomlinson, 1999).
- The needs of exceptionally and profoundly gifted learners can be met through radical adaptations of instructional pacing, including grade skipping and additional subject acceleration.

Educational opportunities for subject and grade skipping must be provided to gifted learners.

Description

Subject acceleration and grade skipping are two forms of acceleration. They may be employed as methods for providing curriculum and services at a level that is matched to a gifted learner's readiness and need. Acceleration is "simply deciding that competence rather than age should be the criterion for determining when an individual obtains access to particular curricula or academic experiences" (Benbow, 1998, p. 281).

Rationale

Gifted learners exhibit advanced intellectual development in one or more areas. Gifted learners come to curricular experiences with knowledge beyond grade-level expectations; therefore, they are entitled to grow from their points of entry (Tomlinson, 1999). Placement in a grade level should be determined by factors other than just age.

Various researchers have shown the importance of nurturing talent development through positive achievement motivation and exposure to increasingly complex tasks. Key concepts and principles, for example, help gifted learners make connections to the topic of study, leading to expanded studies (Tomlinson, 1999).

Benefits

1. Acceleration permits gifted learners to progress at a rate that is commensurate with their readiness and need when they are socially and emotionally ready.
2. Subject and grade skipping are options that allow a gifted learner to be placed at the appropriate instructional level.
3. A flexible system of acceleration provides gifted students with opportunities to progress through the basic curriculum based on mastery of the material.

Potential Barriers

1. Some of greatest opposition to acceleration is from teachers and parents who have reservations about students being moved into higher education at a young age (Gallagher, 1985).
2. Concerns exist regarding the social and emotional development of students who have skipped grades.
3. Subject skipping can create concerns about possible skill gaps.
4. Administrators regard operational feasibility, the translation of an idea into effective practice, as most problematic for implementing these procedures (Gallagher, 1985).
5. Acceleration as a service delivery model often fails to provide the necessary differentiated curriculum for gifted students because the pace and content do not change; the learner simply takes the course at an earlier age (Schiever & Maker, 1989).

Standards and Sample Outcomes

4.0 Minimum Standard	4.0 Exemplary Standard

Decisions to proceed or limit the acceleration of content and grade acceleration must only be considered after a thorough assessment.

- Readiness levels are assessed to determine entry and exit points.
- Gifted learners are placed according to their instructional level given a full understanding of both cognitive and psycho-social development.
- The selection of gifted learners for content and grade acceleration is based on a variety of factors such as general intellectual ability, ability to manipulate abstract symbol systems, intellectual and academic functioning levels, achievement motivation, lack of adjustment problems, and academic readiness (Benbow, 1998).

Possibilities for partial or full acceleration of content and grade levels should be available to any student presenting such needs.

- Teachers seek placement in learning experiences to challenge gifted learners appropriately through complex and abstract curricula.
- Exemplary programming of acceleration includes the additional components of enrichment, counseling, flexible grouping, and individualization.

Learning opportunities for gifted learners must consist of a continuum of differentiated curricular options, instructional approaches, and resource materials.

Description

Differentiated learning experiences for gifted learners specifically consist of planning and implementing varied approaches to content, process, and product modification in response to students' interest, ability levels, readiness, and learning needs (Tomlinson, 1995). Differentiated learning opportunities engage students' differing learning modalities, appeal to interests, vary rates of instruction, and provide a different degree of complexity of content (Tomlinson, 1999). Therefore, an effective approach to programming for gifted learners should be seen as a combination of three elements: accelerative approaches, in which instruction is matched to the competence level of students; enrichment approaches, in which opportunities for the investigation of supplementary material are given; and individualization, in which instruction is matched specifically to the learner's achievement, abilities, and interests (Feldhusen, 1998).

Rationale

Gifted learners require multiple options for taking in information, making sense of ideas, and expressing what they learn (Tomlinson, 1995). Specific strategies for supporting curricular options include: acceleration, ability grouping, high-level curricular materials, career education, and program provisions that influence academic and affective outcomes (Shore & Delcourt, 1996). However, no single format for programming can effectively meet the needs of all gifted learners. Therefore, a continuum of differentiated curricular options, instructional approaches, and resource materials must be available to meet the needs of the diverse learners within the gifted population.

Benefits

1. Multiple approaches to curricular modifications are available to provide the most appropriate curricular experiences for gifted learners.
2. A continuum of differentiated curricular options, instructional approaches, and resource materials supports varying student interests, learning styles, and abilities.

Potential Barriers

1. The pedagogical provisions that are most important for gifted students may not be utilized in actual practice.
2. General education programs emphasize basic skills instruction and may fail to include any appropriate options for gifted learners, let alone a continuum or menu of options.

Standards and Sample Outcomes

5.0 Minimum Standard	5.0 Exemplary Standard

Diverse and appropriate learning experiences must consist of a variety of curricular options, instructional strategies, and materials.

- The criteria for selecting curricular options, instructional strategies, and materials are based on the research regarding appropriateness for gifted learners.

Appropriate service options for each student to work at assessed level(s) and advanced rates of learning should be available.

- Assessment and instruction are inseparable.
- Multiple approaches are available to assess the gifted learners' instructional level so that appropriate service options can be provided.

5.1 Minimum Standard	5.1 Exemplary Standard

Flexible instructional arrangements (e.g., special classes, seminars, resource rooms, mentorships, independent study, and research projects) must be available.

- Flexible instructional arrangements provide a viable means of managing curriculum for gifted learners; they offer opportunities for a differentiated program of studies.

Differentiated educational program curricula for students pre-K–12 should be modified to provide learning experiences matched to students' interests, readiness, and learning styles.

- Different curricular and instructional approaches exist to reflect the varying ways in which gifted learners learn and can demonstrate what they've learned.

6 Professional Development

by Mary S. Landrum, Ph.D.

Gifted learners are entitled to be served by professionals who have specialized preparation in gifted education, expertise in appropriate differentiated content and instructional methods, involvement in ongoing professional development, and who possess exemplary personal and professional traits.

Initial personnel preparation programs are necessary to provide educators with the requisite knowledge base and skills specific to gifted child education. Dependent upon the professional role that an individual plays, the extensiveness of initial training varies. Therefore, ongoing and comprehensive staff development programs in gifted child education are necessary to enhance existing knowledge and skills and to update and make current best practice.

A comprehensive staff development program must be provided for all school staff involved in the education of gifted learners.

Description

Professional development is an ongoing, systemic process. School staff members enter and exit the enduring cycle of professional development activity based on previous knowledge and experience and the need for information as it relates to their professional role in the education of gifted learners.

Rationale

Research indicates that preservice education teachers largely do not develop professional competencies related to gifted education. However, competencies are enhanced following professional development in this area (Tomlinson, Bland, Moon, & Callahan, 1994). Most schools, then, will need to provide teacher training in gifted education through staff development efforts, recognizing that staff have varied professional development needs and enter and exit the staff development program at different points according to their needs and existing knowledge base (Roberts & Roberts, 1986). Quality staff development is an ongoing cyclical process of comprehensive and related efforts, rather than just a succession of unrelated, one-shot in-service activities (Dettmer, 1986). When possible, the staff development program in gifted education should be integrated with overall school or district-based professional development programs and should be a comprehensive set of activities that build on one another in order to meet the staff's varied professional development needs and existing knowledge base (Dettmer & Landrum, 1998).

Benefits

1. Staff members who understand the nature of giftedness and related needs are more sensitive to the plight of gifted learners.
2. Educators knowledgeable about differentiated educational needs and instructional strategies tend to use best practices in their classrooms.
3. Support personnel (e.g., counselors, school psychologists) who understand the particular socio-emotional development of gifted learners modify or adapt their professional practices to accommodate gifted learners.

Potential Barriers

1. Staff development efforts are costly, hence ongoing funding is necessary.
2. Some staff development activities are more time consuming than others.
3. If staff development trainers in gifted education are not readily available, then local leadership must be willing to participate in a trainer-of-trainers approach.
4. Professional development efforts in gifted education that are not embraced by the district-wide staff development program initiatives are seen as secondary or not important.

Standards and Sample Outcomes

1.0 Minimum Standard

All school staff must be made aware of the nature and needs of gifted students.

- Schools provide an in-service on the nature of giftedness and accompanying educational and psychological needs to *all* staff members annually.
- Prior to the implementation of system-wide student identification procedures, school staffs are provided staff development activities related to understanding and recognizing giftedness in the student population.

1.0 Exemplary Standard

All school staff should be provided ongoing staff development in the nature and needs of gifted learners and appropriate instructional strategies.

- Staff development programs in gifted education include a general understanding of giftedness along with related student needs, as well as best practice in nurturing giftedness through effective services as they apply to their roles in the school system.
- Because the knowledge and empirical bases of the field are constantly changing, the content of staff development activities reflect state-of-the-art knowledge and practice.

1.1 Minimum Standard

Teachers of gifted students must attend at least one professional development activity a year designed specifically for teaching gifted learners.

- Teachers attend one of the local professional development opportunities provided annually on topics related to gifted education.
- Teachers attend at least one regional or state professional development event on gifted education each year.

1.1 Exemplary Standard

All teachers of gifted learners should continue to be actively engaged in the study of gifted education through staff development or graduate degree programs.

- Teachers participate in at least one professional development opportunity in gifted education as part of the ongoing certification/licensure renewal program in any given state.
- If a state certification/licensure in gifted education is available and accessible, teachers attend at least one course as part of the certification/licensure renewal program required by the state.
- When new university courses in gifted education are available, teachers complete the courses as part of the certification/licensure renewal program in the state.

Only qualified personnel should be involved in the education of gifted learners.

Description

Gifted education is a specialized field of study. Teaching gifted learners reflects particular knowledge and competencies. Therefore, those who are most qualified to teach gifted learners are those who have participated in a gifted education professional development program. Training may be formal, through a graduate degree program and require obtaining state licensure or certification in graduate coursework, or it may be obtained through more informal training such as institutes and in-service sessions.

Rationale

Research (Moon, Callahan, & Tomlinson, 1999; Tomlinson et al., 1994) findings indicate that persons without training in gifted education are less effective in meeting the particular educational needs of gifted learners. However, novice teachers who were mentored in differentiation for academically diverse student populations have shown improved competencies at managing diverse classroom environments (Moon et al.). Therefore, the person(s) with the primary teaching responsibility for gifted learners must possess the requisite knowledge and competencies. Because gifted education programming should be an extension of good general education curriculum and instruction, qualified teachers in gifted education are first good classroom teachers within their discipline and grade level(s). However, being a good classroom teacher alone is not sufficient for teaching gifted learners.

Benefits

1. The gifted education programming staff takes the lead in applying the pedagogy associated with the field in district-wide administration.
2. Classroom practice is more likely to be consistent with the empirical base from the field of gifted education when led by a knowledgeable professional.

Potential Barriers

1. Access to training in the specialized field of gifted child education is often limited, thereby restricting the candidate pool.
2. Specialized training in gifted child education might be perceived to have a limited vision of the school population and educational programming.

Standards and Sample Outcomes

2.0 Minimum Standard

All personnel working with gifted learners must be certified to teach in the areas to which they are assigned and must be aware of the unique learning differences and needs of gifted learners at the grade level at which they are teaching.

- Staff development in gifted education is integrated into the training provided to specialized school personnel.
- Staff development activities are delivered in strands with specialized information for specific groups of school personnel (e.g., counselors, school psychologists, and so forth).

2.0 Exemplary Standard

All personnel working with gifted learners should participate in regular staff development programs.

- Staff development programs include ongoing activities for all school personnel.
- All staff development activities include follow-up that focuses on specific applications to gifted learners.

2.1 Minimum Standard

All specialist teachers in gifted education must hold or be actively working toward a certification (or the equivalent) in gifted education in the state in which they teach.

- Local training in gifted education can be provided to any staff member interested in gaining this specialized expertise when professional certification is unavailable.
- Teachers working to obtain a licensure in gifted education or its equivalent are supported by the local district with assistance with tuition, time release to complete studies, and so forth.

2.1 Exemplary Standard

All specialist teachers in gifted education should possess a certification/specialization or degree in gifted education.

- Given equal teaching competency, teachers with certification or the equivalent training in gifted education are given priority in filling a job vacancy.

2.2 Minimum Standard	2.2 Exemplary Standard

Any teacher whose primary responsibility for teaching includes gifted learners must have extensive expertise in gifted education.

- Teachers who are selected to teach gifted learners in any discipline or at any grade level have access to training in gifted education or certification in this area when available.
- Teachers with primary responsibility for teaching gifted learners are evaluated to assure their competency in differentiated curricula and instruction.
- Teachers who work with gifted learners, but are without expertise in gifted education, are provided incentives to engage in specialized professional development in a timely manner.

Only teachers with advanced expertise in gifted education should have primary responsibility for the education of gifted learners.

- Given equal teaching competency in general, teachers with advanced knowledge and competence in gifted education are given primary responsibility for gifted learners.
- Teachers without advanced knowledge and competence in gifted education are required to obtain it.

School personnel require support for their specific efforts related to the education of gifted learners.

Description

Most school staff have little or no specialized training in the nature, needs, and instructional strategies specific to the gifted learner population. Therefore, they must participate in professional development activities related to their area of expertise as it applies to gifted learners (Dettmer, 1986).

Rationale

Access to the specific knowledge base and skills necessary to educate gifted learners is typically provided through staff development (Dettmer, 1986). The professional development activities related to gifted education should be integrated into the comprehensive staff development program in the district. This training should not be perceived as an extra activity or add-on to requisite job responsibilities.

Benefits

1. Site-based, integrated staff development programs are accessible to school personnel.
2. All school staff members are aware of the particular characteristics, needs, and nurturing strategies required by gifted learners.
3. Gifted education programming is a collaborative process.

Potential Barriers

1. Departmentalization of responsibilities makes integrated efforts difficult.
2. There may be resistance to integrated staff development programs because of independent goals for staff development.
3. Gifted education training may not be highly prioritized.

Standards and Sample Outcomes

3.0 Minimum Standard	3.0 Exemplary Standard

School personnel must be released from their professional duties to participate in staff development efforts in gifted education.

- Staff development in gifted education should be provided during the regularly scheduled school calendar.
- All staff development activities can include any necessary adaptations or clarifications for use with gifted learners.

Approved staff development activities in gifted education should be funded at least in part by school districts or educational agencies.

- Staff development activities in gifted education are integrated into existing professional development efforts.
- Staff development in gifted education is adequately funded.

The educational staff must be provided with time and other support for the preparation and development of the differentiated education plans, materials, and curricula.

Description

Traditional curriculum and instructional resources are seldom sufficiently supportive of the needs of gifted learners. Therefore, teachers of gifted learners often modify general education materials or develop new ones. Differentiation requires collecting materials from outside of the traditional grade level or school, and it requires access to alternative resources, funds to purchase them, and planning time to develop individualized materials.

Rationale

Gallagher (1999) noted that concert pianists do not have to write their own concertos, however, teachers of gifted learners often must develop their own differentiated educational materials. Unfortunately, the differentiation of educational opportunities requires effort, time, and expertise on the part of the gifted education teacher(s). This type of expertise requires support, including professional development, resource materials, planning time, and access to supplemental materials.

Benefits

1. Materials owned by the district will remain there.
2. Time and resources can alleviate burnout and excess stress caused by the need to differentiate.
3. Supplemental materials must be matched to the core curricula; therefore, they are best developed in-house.

Potential Barriers

1. Materials development is time consuming.
2. Colleagues may view planning and materials-development time as excessive.
3. The cost of supplemental materials is seldom appropriately funded by sources outside of the district.

Standards and Sample Outcomes

4.0 Minimum Standard	4.0 Exemplary Standard
School personnel must be allotted planning time to prepare for the differentiated education of gifted learners.	*Regularly scheduled planning time (e.g., release time, summer pay, etc.) should be allotted to teachers for the development of differentiated educational programs and related resources.*

- The ongoing differentiation of the core curriculum for gifted learners is prepared regularly.
- Teachers who use supplemental teaching resources are given time for planning differentiated lessons either during the academic year or through summer support.

- School staff are released during the school year or paid to meet during times off-contract to conduct long-term planning for differentiation for gifted learners.
- Teachers develop differentiated curriculum units during noncontract hours for additional pay.

7 Program Evaluation

by Carolyn M. Callahan, Ph.D.

Program evaluation is the systematic study of the value and impact of services provided.

The effectiveness of services to gifted students is likely to be improved if decisions about the development of all program components are guided by careful decision making based on valid and reliable evidence of what works and what does not work across all the major aspects of program operation. Hence, the most robust provisions for gifted learners will evolve from careful collection of data regarding the context in which the services are delivered, the adequacy and appropriateness of resources available, the quality of activities carried out, and finally, the degree to which goals and objectives have been achieved.

An evaluation must be purposeful.

Description

In designing evaluations that will help improve service quality, we must have a clear idea of the kinds of questions and data that are important to the stakeholders—those people who will use the information we are collecting. We must address the important questions and issues—those that will guide good decision making. Thus, it is important to decide on the important evaluation questions and how decision makers will use the evaluation results. An evaluation that collects data that no one is interested in or answers questions that no one cared about is a waste of program resources.

Rationale

Program evaluation is an expensive enterprise in terms of money, as well as the time and energy of personnel. The critical outcomes of the expenditure are information and recommendations that are openly received by the audiences who make decisions relative to the program. Early identification and continued involvement of audiences is more likely to lead to acceptance of evaluation recommendations (Joint Committee on Standards for Educational Evaluation, 1994; Reineke, 1991; Tomlinson, Bland, & Moon, 1993; Tomlinson, Bland, Moon, & Callahan, 1994; Tomlinson & Callahan, 1993). In particular, Tomlinson et al. (1994) found clear evaluation purposes and involvement of a wider representative group in planning and implementation to characterize stronger and more effective evaluation designs and great utilization of results.

Benefits

1. With a clear purpose and rationale, the money and time expended on evaluation are most likely to yield data that can and will be used for proactive decision making.
2. Key decision makers will be able to see the impact of program services in terms of clearly defined outcomes.
3. Key decision makers are more likely to look at evaluation results as formative (directed toward improving program services), rather than simply as summative (judging overall worth of the program or success in achieving outcomes).

Potential Barriers

1. Program services that are not clearly delineated or that do not have clearly specified goals and objectives will result in difficulty deciding on important questions and issues.
2. Stakeholders who are not actively involved in and informed about program activities are likely left out of the evaluation process, as well.
3. If the evaluation threatens those closest to the program, they may seek to divert the evaluation process toward the innocuous and trivial.

Standards and Sample Outcomes

1.0 Minimum Standard	1.0 Exemplary Standard
Information collected must reflect the interests and needs of most of the constituency groups.	*Information collected should address pertinent questions raised by all constituency groups and should be responsive to the needs of all stakeholders.*

- Representatives of parent, teacher, administrator, student, school board, and community groups are surveyed to identify issues of concern.

- Representatives of parent, teacher, administrator, student, school board, and community groups are brought together to identify the focus of the evaluation and to prioritize the key evaluation questions.
- Representatives of all groups maintain an active role in reviewing the process of designing data collection tools, in advising on appropriate informants for interviews, and in distributing and explaining evaluation results.

An evaluation must be efficient and economic.

Description

The collection of evaluation data should be directed toward answering the most important evaluation questions in ways that require the least amount of time, money, and effort, but not at the expense of collecting valid and reliable information that will lead to good decision making. This may mean sampling instead of surveying all students or parents in a school district, or it may mean deciding to answer several evaluation questions through one survey instead of multiple surveys. However, it also means rejecting the use of data from standardized tests that are routinely administered in the school district, but do not reflect program goals.

Rationale

The Joint Committee on Standards for Educational Evaluation (1994) noted that common errors that mitigate against the production of useful evaluations include: (1) commencing an evaluation without allocating sufficient funds to complete it; (2) choosing a methodology because of cost concerns, rather than because it will lead to the most useful and important data collection; and (3) changing an evaluation plan without making necessary budget changes.

Benefits

1. Limited resources are expended most judiciously. Maximum effort is made to ensure that time and energy of personnel are reserved for critical functions in delivering services to gifted students.
2. Cooperation of informants is enhanced when they perceive the evaluators are respectful of their time and that they are providing important and nonredundant information.

Potential Barriers

1. Planning that does not prioritize evaluation questions and carefully identify appropriate sources of information may result in the collection of data from sources that do not have access to, or are not informed about, the issues they are asked to address.
2. Use of inappropriate data collection tools, because they are convenient, may result in not being able to address the real evaluation questions. For example, asking teachers what they do instead of observing what they do may result in invalid assessments of the differentiation of curriculum.

Standards and Sample Outcomes

2.0 Minimum Standard	2.0 Exemplary Standard

School districts must provide sufficient resources for program evaluation.

- The district determines the most critical evaluation questions and allocates local resources to the collection of data relevant to those questions.

School districts should allocate adequate time, financial support, and personnel to conduct systematic program evaluation.

- The school district establishes a plan for regular, comprehensive evaluation across all program components.
- The school division uses an external evaluator to gather information that cannot be reliably or validly collected internally.

An evaluation must be conducted competently and ethically.

Description

The successful completion of an evaluation study is highly dependent on the skills and professional code of right and wrong of the evaluator(s). The skills range from the general skills of communication and negotiation to specific skills in designing and implementing evaluation studies and knowledge of standards for gifted programs. Further, evaluations deal with sensitive data and high-stakes outcomes for students, teachers, and administrators. In order to protect these individuals both in the data collection and the effects the evaluation has on their lives, the evaluator(s) must know, respect, and apply principles of privacy and protection of human subjects and also make every effort not to allow personal bias to influence the process. In any case, all potential biases should be made public as the evaluator begins his or her involvement with the schools.

Rationale

A study of evaluation utilization in gifted education found that the stronger evaluations with results that were more fully utilized were characterized by either teams where there was expertise in both program evaluation and gifted education or where those traits characterized the individual in charge of designing and implementing the program evaluation (Tomlinson et al., 1994).

Benefits

1. Competence in evaluation planning and implementation will be the basis for valid and reliable outcomes.
2. Confidence in the competence and trustworthiness of evaluators will result in full disclosure by informants.
3. Results are most likely to result in improvement of services to gifted students with minimum threat to individuals.

Potential Barriers

1. Evaluators without expertise in gifted education may lack an understanding of the needs of the population and lack an understanding of criteria for appropriate services.
2. Evaluators with a background in gifted education, but not in evaluation design and implementation, may lack the skills in producing credible, reliable, and valid information.
3. Evaluators with a particular bias about programming strategies or curriculum for the gifted may judge according to personal standards, rather than the standards of the school district or the field of gifted education.

Standards and Sample Outcomes

3.0 Minimum Standard

Persons conducting the evaluation must be competent and trustworthy.

- Respondents to questionnaires and interviews are open and forthright in responding in the data-collection phase because the surveys and interview protocols are carefully developed.
- Data will be collected that responds to the critical and important evaluation questions.

3.0 Exemplary Standard

Persons conducting the evaluation should possess an expertise in program evaluation in gifted education.

- The recommendations offered for improving services reflect an understanding of the issues and goals of providing quality, differentiated education for gifted learners.
- Recommendations reflect sensitivity to the political issues surrounding gifted education.

3.1 Minimum Standard

The program evaluation design must address whether or not services have reached intended goals.

- The evaluation results are focused on concerns that go beyond process data to address whether the services are having the desired impact on the learning, performance, and affective outcomes expected as a result of the investment of resources in the delivery of services.

3.1 Exemplary Standard

The evaluation design should report the strengths and weaknesses found in the program, as well as critical issues that might influence program services.

- The decision makers examine the resources and activities of the program in order to attribute the outcome results to specific processes and inputs that were part of the delivery of services.
- The evaluation report serves as a clear guide for administration and teachers on areas where changes can be made to improve the program.

Standards and Sample Outcomes continued

3.2 Minimum Standard	3.2 Exemplary Standard

Instruments and procedures used for data collection must be valid and reliable for their intended use.

Care should be taken to ensure that instruments with sufficient evidence of reliability and validity are used and that they are appropriate for varying age, developmental levels, gender, and diversity of the target population.

- The data collected represent credible assessments of program outcomes and activities.
- Outcomes are attributed to the delivery of services, rather than halo effects, other educational services, or random error in assessment.

- Parents who are not English-language speakers or readers have equal opportunity to be addressed in the data-collection process.
- Students are not frustrated by tasks beyond their developmental range; yet, ceiling effects that may result in under estimation of program effects are avoided.

3.3 Minimum Standard	3.3 Exemplary Standard

Ongoing formative and summative evaluation strategies must be used for substantive program improvement and development.

Formative evaluations should be conducted regularly with summative evaluations occurring minimally every five years or more often as specified by state or local district policies.

- Program services are modified as data provide suggestions and recommendations for improving the process of delivering services in ways that will have positive impacts on students.
- Ineffective and inefficient program services are modified or eliminated.

- Regularly scheduled evaluations reduce the threats and fears that come with sporadic and unpredictable evaluations. The evaluation process is part of program operations.
- Practices that are inefficient and ineffective are identified and changed before they become entrenched to the degree that staff feel they must defend them.
- Regular program evaluation permits curriculum and operational practice to be regularly updated with current theory and research.

Standards and Sample Outcomes continued

3.4 Minimum Standard	3.4 Exemplary Standard
Individual data must be held confidential.	*All individuals who are involved in the evaluation process should be given the opportunity to verify information and the resulting interpretation.*

- Personal privacy is maintained and respondents come to trust the process.

- Errors of bias, which may effect the selection of data to report from interviews, are avoided.
- Informants are satisfied that they have had the opportunity to clarify, correct, and expand upon information they have provided, adding credibility to reports.

The evaluation results must be made available through a written report.

Description

The effective presentation of findings and recommendations will require communication via a number of vehicles and to a number of audiences. The audience's level of sophistication, interests, and decision-making responsibility will influence the choice of presentation style. However, a written document is needed to serve as the "memory" of those who hear the report and as a source for verification and clarification of oral presentation. The format of the written report should be such that it is easily accessible and readable for the audiences who will use it for decision making.

Rationale

In receiving evaluation reports, the stakeholders or primary interest groups may be sensitive to results that either confirm or refute strongly held feelings and may filter results according to those sensitivities. Accordingly, it is important that a document exist to provide a reference point for clarity. Further, not all audiences will have the same background about the program or the same understanding of technical and statistical jargon and methodology. Hence, it is critical that there be multiple reporting strategies designed to communicate effectively to all interested audiences (Joint Committee on Standards for Educational Evaluation, 1994; Lincoln, 1991).

Benefits

1. Documents exist for immediate referral and also for long-term planning.
2. As program changes are made, the written report can serve as an anchor for comparison as data is collected over time through subsequent formative and summative evaluations.
3. All stakeholders have access to the same information.
4. Cooperation of informants is enhanced when they perceive that the evaluators will be sharing the evaluation report with all.

Potential Barriers

1. In haste to deliver final reports, the evaluators rely only on written documents, and those documents are prepared in technical formats that are only understood by other evaluators.
2. Too much emphasis is put on methodology, rather than interpretations and recommendations, because of a lack of understanding of gifted program options and curriculum.
3. Stakeholders focus on the negative in the report, rather than the full scope of findings.

Standards and Sample Outcomes

4.0 Minimum Standard	4.0 Exemplary Standard

Evaluation reports must present the evaluation results in a clear and cohesive format.

- The language of the evaluation report reflects the audience(s) and, hence, is understood by the stakeholders.
- Opportunities for interpretation according to political agendas of constituencies are minimized.

Evaluation reports should be designed to present results and encourage follow-through by stakeholders.

- Evaluation reports are treated as action documents to guide program development.
- Individuals within the school division are able to determine the best way to proceed with program revisions, including financial, staffing, operation, and curricular and instructional modifications.
- Individuals within each stakeholder group understand his or her role in program development.

References

Achter, J. A., Benbow, C. P., & Lubinski, D. (1997). Rethinking multipotentiality among the intellectually gifted: A critical review and recommendations. *Gifted Child Quarterly, 41*, 5–15.

Alvino, J. (1991). An investigation into the needs of gifted boys. *Roeper Review, 13*, 174–180.

Archambault, Jr., F. X., Westberg, K. L., Brown, S W., Hallmark, B W., Zhang, W., & Emmons, C. L. (1993). Classroom practices used with gifted third and fourth grade students. *Journal for the Education of the Gifted, 16,* 103–119.

Bands, C. (1989). Promoting pluralism and power. In C. J. Maker & S. W. Schiever (Eds.), *Critical issues in gifted education: Defensible programs for cultural and ethnic minorities* (pp. 27–33). Austin, TX: PRO-ED.

Benbow, C. P. (1998). Acceleration as a method for meeting the academic needs of intellectually talented children. In J. VanTassel-Baska (Ed.), *Excellence in educating gifted and talented learners* (pp. 279–294). Denver, CO: Love.

Borland, J. D. (1989). *Planning and implementing programs for the gifted.* New York: Teachers College Press.

Callahan, C. M., Landrum, M. S., & Hunsaker, S. L. (1988*). Suggestions for program development, revision and extension in gifted education.* Richmond, VA: Department of Education, Division of Special Education Programs.

Callahan, C. M., & McIntire, J. (1994). Identifying outstanding talent in American Indians and Alaska Native students. Washington, DC: Office of Educational Research and Improvement.

Colangelo, N. (1997). Counseling gifted students: Issues and practices. In N. Colangelo & G. A. Davis (Eds.), *Handbook of gifted education* (2nd ed.; pp. 353–365). New York: Allyn and Bacon.

Cox, J., Daniel, N. & Boston, B. A. (1985). *Educating able learners: Programs and promising practices.* Austin, TX: University of Texas Press.

Davis, G. A., & Rimm, S. B. (1998). *Education of the gifted and talented.* Boston: Allyn and Bacon.

Delcourt, M. A. B., & Evans, K. (1994). *Qualitative extension of the learning outcomes study*. Storrs, CT: University of Connecticut, National Research Center on the Gifted and Talented.

Delcourt, J., Loyd, B., Cornell, D., & Goldberg, M. (1994). *Evaluation of the effects of programming arrangements on student learning outcomes*. Storrs, CT: University of Connecticut, National Research Center on the Gifted and Talented.

Delisle, J. (1992). *Guiding the social and emotional development of gifted youth*. New York: Longman

Dettmer, P. (1986). Gifted program in-service and staff development: Pragmatics and possibilities. *Gifted Child Quarterly, 30*, 99–102.

Dettmer, P., & Landrum, M. S. (1998*). Staff development: The key for effective gifted education programs*. Waco, TX: Prufrock Press.

Feldhusen, J. F. (1998). Strategies and methods for teaching the talented. In J. VanTassel-Baska (Ed.), *Excellence in educating gifted and talented learners* (pp. 363–379). Denver, CO: Love.

Ford, D. Y. (1998). The under-representation of minority students in gifted education: Problems and promises in recruitment and retention. *Journal of Special Education, 32*, 4–14.

Ford, D. Y. (1996). *Reversing underachievement among gifted Black students*. New York: Teachers College Press.

Gallagher, J. J (1999, November). *Gifted education in the new millennium*. Paper presented at the annual conference of the National Association for Gifted Children, Albuquerque, NM.

Gallagher, J. J. (1985). *Teaching the gifted child*. Boston: Allyn and Bacon.

Gallagher, J. J., & Gallagher, S. (1994). *Teaching the gifted child*. Boston: Allyn and Bacon.

Johnson, L. J., Karnes, M. B., & Carr, V. W. (1997). Providing services to children with gifts and dis-abilities: A critical need. In N. Colangelo & G. A. Davis (Eds.), *Handbook of gifted education* (2nd ed.; pp. 516–527). New York: Allyn and Bacon.

Joint Committee on Standards for Educational Evaluation. (1994). *The program evaluation standards* (2nd ed.). Thousand Oaks, CA: Sage.

Kerr, B. A. (1991*). A handbook for counseling the gifted and talented*. Alexandria, VA: American Association for Counseling and Development.

Kirschenbaum, R. J., Armstrong, D. C., & Landrum, M. S. (1999). Resource consultation model in gifted education to support talent development in today's inclusive schools. *Gifted Child Quarterly, 43*, 39–47.

Landrum, M. S., & Shaklee, B. (Eds.). (1998). *Pre-K–Grade 12 gifted program standards*. Washington, DC: National Association for Gifted Children.

Lincoln, Y. S. (1991). The arts and sciences of program evaluation. *Evaluation Practice, 12*, 1–7.

Maker, C. J. (1996). Identification of gifted minority students: A national problem, needed changes, and a promising solution. *Gifted Child Quarterly, 40*, 41–50.

Maker, C. J. (1982). *Teaching models in the education of the gifted*. Austin, TX: PRO-ED.

Masse, L., & Gagné, F. (1996). Should self-nominations be allowed in peer nomination forms? *Gifted Child Quarterly, 40*, 24–30.

Maxwell, E. (1998). "I can do it myself:" Reflections on early self-efficacy. *Roeper Review, 20,* 193–187.

McIntosh, M. E., & Greenlaw, M. J. (1986). Fostering the post-secondary aspirations of gifted urban minority students. *Roeper Review, 9,* 104–107.

Mendaglio, S., & Pyryt, M. C. (1995). Self-concept of gifted students: Assessment-based intervention. *Teaching Exceptional Children, 27,* 40–45.

Moon, T. R., Callahan, C. M., & Tomlinson, C. A. (1999). The effects of mentoring relationships on preservice teachers' attitudes toward academically diverse students. *Gifted Child Quarterly, 43,* 56–62.

Neihart, M. (1999). Systematic risk-taking. *Roeper Review, 21,* 289–292.

Olszewski-Kubilius, P. M., & Scott, J. M. (1992). An investigation of the college and career counseling needs of economically disadvantaged, minority gifted students. *Roeper Review, 14,* 141–148.

Piechowski, M. M. (1997). Emotional giftedness: The measure of intrapersonal intelligence. In N. Colangelo & G. A. Davis (Eds.), *Handbook of gifted education* (2nd ed.; pp. 366–381). New York: Allyn and Bacon.

Purcell, J. (1994). *The status of programs for high ability students*. Storrs, CT: University of Connecticut, National Research Center on the Gifted and Talented.

Purcell, J. H., & Leppien, J. H. (1998). Building bridges between general practitioners and educators of the gifted: A study of collaboration. *Gifted Child Quarterly, 42,* 172–180.

Reineke, R. A. (1991). Stakeholder involvement in evaluation: Suggestions for practice. *Evaluation Practice, 12,* 39–44.

Reis, S. M. (1991). The need for clarification in research designed to examine differences in achievement and accomplishment. *Roeper Review, 13,* 193–198.

Reis, S. M., Burns, D. E., & Renzulli, J. S. (1992). *Curriculum compacting: The complete guide to modifying the regular curriculum for high ability students*. Mansfield Center, CT: Creative Learning Press.

Renzulli, J. S., & Reis, S. (1991). The reform movement and the quiet crisis in gifted education. *Gifted Child Quarterly, 35,* 26–35.

Roberts, J. L., & Roberts, R. A. (1986). Differentiating in-service through teacher concerns about education of the gifted. *Gifted Child Quarterly 30,* 107–109.

Robinson, A. (1997). Cooperative learning for talented students: Emergent issues and implications. In N. Colangelo & G. A. Davis (Eds.), *A handbook of gifted education* (2nd ed.; pp. 243–252). Boston: Allyn and Bacon.

Robinson, N. W., & Noble, K. D. (1991). Social-emotional development and adjustment of gifted children. In M. Wang, M. C. Reynolds, & H. J. Walberg (Eds.), *Handbook of special education: Research and practice* (2nd ed.; pp. 57–76). New York: Pergamon Press.

Roedell, W. C. (1989). Early development of gifted children. J. L. VanTassel-Baska & P. Olszewski-Kubilius (Eds.), *Patterns of influence on gifted learners* (pp. 13–28). New York: Teacher's College Press.

Rogers, J. A. (1998). Refocusing the lens: Using observation to assess and identify gifted learners. *Gifted Education International, 12,* 129–144.

Schiever, J. W., & Maker, C. J. (Eds.). (1989). *Defensible programs for cultural and ethnic minorities.* Austin, TX: PRO-ED.

Shaklee, B. (1997). Gifted-child education in the new millennium. *The Educational Forum, 61,* 212–219.

Shore, B. M., & Delcourt, M. A. B. (1996). Effective curricular and program practices in gifted education and the interface with general education. *Journal for the Education of the Gifted, 20,* 138–154.

Silverman, L. K. (1993). The gifted individual. In L. K. Silverman (Ed.), *Counseling the gifted and talented* (pp. 3–28). Denver, CO: Love.

Tomlinson, C. A. (1999). *The differentiated classroom: Responding to the needs of all learners.* Alexandria, VA: Association for Supervision and Curriculum Development.

Tomlinson, C. A. (1995). *How to differentiate instruction in mixed-ability classrooms.* Alexandria, VA: Association for Supervision and Curriculum Development.

Tomlinson, C. A., Bland, L., & Moon, T. (1993). Evaluation utilization: A review of the literature with implications for gifted education. *Journal for the Education of the Gifted, 16,* 171–189.

Tomlinson, C. A., Bland, L., Moon, T., & Callahan, C. M. (1994). Case studies of evaluation utilization in gifted education. *Evaluation Practice, 15,* 153–168.

Tomlinson, C. A., & Callahan, C. M. (1993, Fall). A planning guide for evaluating programs for the gifted. *Quest, 4*(2), 1–4.

Tomlinson, C. A., Coleman, M. R., Allan, S. D., Udall, A., & Landrum, M. S. (1996). Interface between gifted education and general education: Toward communication, cooperation, and collaboration. *Gifted Child Quarterly, 40,* 165–171.

Tomlinson, C. A., Tomchin, E. M., Callahan, C. M., Adams, C. M., Pizzat-Tinnin, P., Cunningham, C. M., Moore, B., Lutz, L., Roberson, C., Eiss, N., Landrum, M. S., Hunsaker, S. L., & Imbeau, M. (1994). Practices of preservice teachers related to gifted and other academically diverse learners. *Gifted Child Quarterly, 38,* 106–114.

U.S. Department of Education, Office of educational Research and Improvement. (1993). *National excellence: A case for developing America's talent.* Washington, DC: U.S. Goverment Printing Office.

VanTassel-Baska, J. (1998). Appropriate curriculum for the talented learner. In J. VanTassel-Baska (Ed.), *Excellence in educating gifted and talented learners* (pp. 339–361). Denver, CO: Love.

VanTassel-Baska, J. (1994). *Comprehensive curriculum for gifted learners.* Boston: Love.

VanTassel-Baska, J. (1992). *Planning effective curriculum for gifted learners.* Denver, CO: Love.

Westberg, K. L., Archambault, F. X. Jr., Dobyns, S. M., & Slavin, T. J. (1993). An observational study of classroom practices used with third and fourth grade students. *Journal for the Education of the Gifted, 16,* 120–146.

Worthern, B. R., Sanders, J. R., & Fitzpatrick, J. L. (1997). *Program evaluation: Alternative approaches and practical guidelines* (2nd ed.). New York: Longman.

Appendix

Pre-K–Grade 12 Gifted Program Standards

Gifted Education Programming Criterion: Program Design

Description: The development of appropriate gifted education programming requires comprehensive services based on sound philosophical, theoretical, and empirical support.

Guiding Principles		Minimum Standards		Exemplary Standards
1. Rather than any single gifted program, a continuum of programming services must exist for gifted learners.	1.0M	Gifted programming services must be accessible to all gifted learners.	1.0E	Levels of services should be matched to the needs of gifted learners by providing a full continuum of options.
2. Gifted education must be adequately funded.	2.0M	Gifted education funding should be equitable compared to the funding of other local programming.	2.0E	Gifted education programming must receive funding consistent with the program goals and sufficient to adequately meet them.
3. Gifted education programming must evolve from a comprehensive and sound base.	3.0M	Gifted education programming must be submitted for outside review on a regular basis.	3.0E	Gifted education programming should be planned as a result of consultation with informed experts.
	3.1M	Gifted programming must be guided by a clearly articulated philosophy statement and accompanying goals and objectives.	3.1E	The school or school district should have a mission/philosophy statement that addresses the need for gifted education programming.
	3.2M	A continuum of services must be provided across grades pre-K–12.	3.2E	A comprehensive pre-K–12 program plan should include policies and procedures for identification, curriculum and instruction, service delivery, teacher preparation, formative and summative evaluation, support services, and parent involvement.
4. Gifted education programming services must be an integral part of the general education school day.	4.0M	Gifted education programming should be articulated with the general education program.	4.0E	Gifted services must be designed to supplement and build on the basic academic skills and knowledge learned in regular classrooms at all grade levels to ensure continuity as students progress through the program.

5. Flexible groupings of students must be developed in order to facilitate differentiated instruction and curriculum.

6. Policies specific to adapting and adding to the nature and operations of the general education program are necessary for gifted education.

4.1M Appropriate educational opportunities must be provided in the regular classroom, resource classroom, separate, or optional voluntary environments.

5.0M The use of flexible grouping of gifted learners must be an integral part of gifted education programming.

6.0M Existing and future school policies must include provisions for the needs of gifted learners.

4.1E Local school districts should offer multiple service delivery options as no single service should stand alone.

5.0E Gifted learners should be included in flexible grouping arrangements in all content areas and grade levels to ensure that gifted students learn with and from intellectual peers.

6.0E Gifted education policies should exist for at least the following areas: early entrance, grade skipping, ability grouping, and dual enrollment.

Gifted Education Programming Criterion: Program Administration and Management

Description: Appropriate gifted education programming must include the establishment of a systematic means of developing, implementing, and managing services.

Guiding Principles	Minimum Standards	Exemplary Standards
1. Appropriately qualified personnel must direct services for the education of gifted learners.	1.0M The designated coordinator of gifted education programming must have completed coursework or staff development in gifted education and display leadership ability to be deemed appropriately qualified.	1.0E The designated gifted programming coordinator must have completed a certification program or advanced degree program in gifted education.
2. Gifted education programming must be integrated into the general education program.	2.0M The gifted education program must create linkages between general education and gifted education at all levels.	2.0E Responsibility for the education of gifted learners is a shared one requiring strong relationships between the gifted education program and general education schoolwide.
3. Gifted education programming must include positive working relationships with constituency and advocacy groups, as well as with compliance agencies.	3.0M Gifted programming staff must establish ongoing parent communication.	3.0E The gifted education programming staff should facilitate the dissemination of information regarding major policies and practices in gifted education (e.g., student referral and screening, appeals, informed consent, student progress, etc.) to school personnel, parents, community members, etc.
	3.1M Gifted programs must establish and use an advisory committee that reflects the cultural and socioeconomic diversity of the school or school district's total student population and includes parents, community members, students, and school staff members.	3.1E Parents of gifted learners should have regular opportunities to share input and make recommendations about program operations with the gifted programming coordinator.

3.2M Gifted education programming staff must communicate with other on-site departments, as well as other educational agencies vested in the education of gifted learners (e.g., other school districts, school board members, state departments of education, intermediate educational agencies, etc.).

3.2E The gifted education program should consider current issues and concerns from other educational fields and agencies regarding gifted programming decision making on a regular basis.

4. Requisite resources and materials must be provided to support the efforts of gifted education programming.

4.0M Resources must be provided to support program operations.

4.0E A diversity of resources (e.g., parent, community, vocational, etc.) should be available to support program operations.

4.1M Technological support must be provided for gifted education programming services.

4.1E Gifted education programming should provide state-of-the-art technology to support appropriate services.

4.2M The library selections must reflect a range of materials including those appropriate for gifted learners.

4.2E The acquisition plan for purchasing new materials for the school should reflect the needs of gifted learners.

Gifted Education Programming Criterion: Socio-Emotional Guidance and Counseling

Description: Gifted education programming must establish a plan to recognize and nurture the unique socio-emotional development of gifted learners.

Guiding Principles	Minimum Standards	Exemplary Standards
1. Gifted learners must be provided with differentiated guidance efforts to meet their unique socio-emotional development.	1.0M Gifted learners, because of their unique socio-emotional development, must be provided with guidance and counseling services by a counselor who is familiar with the characteristics and socio-emotional needs of gifted learners.	1.0E Counseling services should be provided by a counselor familiar with specific training in the characteristics and socio-emotional needs (i.e., underachievement, multipotentiality, etc.) of diverse gifted learners.
2. Gifted learners must be provided with career guidance services especially designed for their unique needs.	2.0M Gifted learners must be provided with career guidance consistent with their unique strengths.	2.0E Gifted learners should be provided with college and career guidance that is appropriately different and delivered earlier than typical programs.
3. Gifted at-risk students must be provided with guidance and counseling to help them reach their potential.	3.0M Gifted learners who are at risk must have special attention, counseling, and support to help them realize their full potential.	3.0E Gifted learners who do not demonstrate satisfactory performance in regular and/or gifted education classes should be provided with specialized intervention services.
4. Gifted learners must be provided with affective curriculum in addition to differentiated guidance and counseling services.	4.0M Gifted learners must be provided with affective curriculum as part of differentiated curriculum and instructional services.	4.0E A well-defined and implemented affective curriculum scope and sequence containing personal/social awareness and adjustment, academic planning, and vocational and career awareness should be provided to gifted learners.

5. Underachieving gifted learners must be served, rather than omitted from differentiated services.

5.0M Gifted students who are under-achieving must not be exited from gifted programs because of related problems.

5.0E Underachieving gifted learners should be provided with specific guidance and counseling services that address the issues and problems related to underachievement.

Gifted Education Programming Criterion: Student Identification

Description: Gifted learners must be assessed to determine appropriate educational services.

Guiding Principles	Minimum Standards	Exemplary Standards
1. A comprehensive and cohesive process for student nomination must be coordinated in order to determine eligibility for gifted education services.	1.0M Information regarding the characteristics of gifted students in areas served by the district must be annually disseminated to all appropriate staff members.	1.0E The school district should provide information annually, in a variety of languages, regarding the process for nominating students for gifted education programming services.
	1.1M All students must comprise the initial screening pool of potential recipients of gifted education services.	1.1E The nomination process should be ongoing, and screening of any student should occur at any time.
	1.2M Nominations for services must be accepted from any source (e.g., teachers, parents, community members, peers, etc.).	1.2E Nomination procedures and forms should be available in a variety of languages.
	1.3M Parents must be provided with information regarding an understanding of giftedness and student characteristics.	1.3E Parents should be provided with special workshops or seminars to gain a full meaning of giftedness.
2. Instruments used for student assessment to determine eligibility for gifted education services must measure diverse abilities, talents, strengths, and needs in order to provide students an opportunity to demonstrate any strengths.	2.0M Assessment instruments must measure the capabilities of students with provisions for the language in which the student is most fluent, when available.	2.0E Assessments should be provided in a language in which the student is most fluent, if available.
	2.1M Assessments must be culturally fair.	2.1E Assessment should be responsive to students' economic conditions, gender, developmental differences, handicapping conditions, and other factors that mitigate against fair assessment practices.

2.2E Students identified in all designated areas of giftedness within a school district should be assessed consistently across grade levels.

2.3E Student assessments should be sensitive to all stages of talent development.

3.0E Individual assessment plans should be developed for all gifted learners who need gifted education.

3.1E An assessment profile should reflect the gifted learner's interests, learning style, and educational needs.

4.0E Student assessment data should come from multiple sources and include multiple assessment methods.

4.1E Student assessment data should represent an appropriate balance of reliable and valid quantitative and qualitative measures.

5.0E Student placement data should be collected using an appropriate balance of quantitative and qualitative measures with adequate evidence of reliability and validity for the purposes of identification.

5.1E District guidelines and procedures should be reviewed and revised when necessary.

2.2M The purpose(s) of student assessments must be consistently articulated across all grade levels.

2.3M Student assessments must be sensitive to the current stage of talent development.

3. A student assessment profile of individual strengths and needs must be developed to plan appropriate intervention.

3.0M An assessment profile must be developed for each child to evaluate eligibility for gifted education programming services.

3.1M An assessment profile must reflect the unique learning characteristics and potential and performance levels.

4. All student identification procedures and instruments must be based on current theory and research.

4.0M No single assessment instrument or its results denies student eligibility for gifted programming services.

4.1M All assessment instruments must provide evidence of reliability and validity for the intended purposes and target students.

5. Written procedures for student identification must include, at the very least, provisions for informed consent, student retention, student reassessment, student exiting, and appeals procedures.

5.0M District gifted programming guidelines must contain specific procedures for student assessment at least once during the elementary, middle, and secondary levels.

5.1M District guidelines must provide specific procedures for student retention and exiting, as well as guidelines for parent appeals.

Gifted Education Programming Criterion: Curriculum and Instruction

Description: Gifted education services must include curricular and instructional opportunities directed to the unique needs of the gifted learner.

Guiding Principles

1. Differentiated curriculum for the gifted learner must span grades pre–K–12.

2. Regular classroom curricula and instruction must be adapted, modified, or replaced to meet the unique needs of gifted learners.

Minimum Standards

1.0M Differentiated curriculum (curricular and instructional adaptations that address the unique learning needs of gifted learners) for gifted learners must be integrated and articulated throughout the district.

2.0M Instruction, objectives, and strategies provided to gifted learners must be systematically differentiated from those in the regular classroom.

2.1M Teachers must differentiate, replace, supplement, or modify curricula to facilitate higher level learning goals.

2.2M Means for demonstrating proficiency in essential regular curriculum concepts and processes must be established to facilitate appropriate academic acceleration.

2.3M Gifted learners must be assessed for proficiency in basic skills and knowledge and provided with alternative challenging educational opportunities when proficiency is demonstrated.

Exemplary Standards

1.0E A well-defined and implemented curriculum scope and sequence should be articulated for all grade levels and all subject areas.

2.0E District curriculum plans should include objectives, content, and resources that challenge gifted learners in the regular classroom.

2.1E Teachers should be responsible for developing plans to differentiate the curriculum in every discipline for gifted learners.

2.2E Documentation of instruction for assessing level(s) of learning and accelerated rates of learning should demonstrate plans for gifted learners based on specific needs of individual learners.

2.3E Gifted learners should be assessed for proficiency in all standard courses of study and subsequently provided with more challenging educational opportunities.

3. Instructional pace must be flexible to allow for the accelerated learning of gifted learners as appropriate.

3.0M A program of instruction must consist of advanced content and appropriately differentiated teaching strategies to reflect the accelerative learning pace and advanced intellectual processes of gifted learners.

3.0E When warranted, continual opportunities for curricular acceleration should be provided in gifted learners' areas of strength and interest while allowing a sufficient ceiling for optimal learning.

4. Educational opportunities for subject and grade skipping must be provided to gifted learners.

4.0M Decisions to proceed or limit the acceleration of content and grade acceleration must only be considered after a thorough assessment.

4.0E Possibilities for partial or full acceleration of content and grade levels should be available to any student presenting such needs.

5. Learning opportunities for gifted learners must consist of a continuum of differentiated curricular options, instructional approaches, and resource materials.

5.0M Diverse and appropriate learning experiences must consist of a variety of curricular options, instructional strategies, and materials.

5.1M Flexible instructional arrangements (e.g., special classes, seminars, resource rooms, mentorships, independent study, and research projects) must be available.

5.0E Appropriate service options for each student to work at assessed level(s) and advanced rates of learning should be available.

5.1E Differentiated educational program curricula for students pre-K–12 should be modified to provide learning experiences matched to students' interests, readiness, and learning styles.

Gifted Education Programming Criterion: Professional Development

Description: Gifted learners are entitled to be served by professionals who have specialized preparation in gifted education, expertise in appropriate differentiated content and instructional methods, involvement in ongoing professional development, and who possess exemplary personal and professional traits.

Guiding Principles	Minimum Standards	Exemplary Standards
1. A comprehensive staff development program must be provided for all school staff involved in the education of gifted learners.	1.0M All school staff must be made aware of the nature and needs of gifted students.	1.0E All school staff should be provided ongoing staff development in the nature and needs of gifted learners and appropriate instructional strategies.
	1.1M Teachers of gifted students must attend at least one professional development activity a year designed specifically for teaching gifted learners.	1.1E All teachers of gifted learners should continue to be actively engaged in the study of gifted education through staff development or graduate degree programs.
2. Only qualified personnel should be involved in the education of gifted learners.	2.0M All personnel working with gifted learners must be certified to teach in the areas to which they are assigned and must be aware of the unique learning differences and needs of gifted learners at the grade level at which they are teaching.	2.0E All personnel working with gifted learners should participate in regular staff development programs.
	2.1M All specialist teachers in gifted education must hold or be actively working toward a certification (or the equivalent) in gifted education in the state in which they teach.	2.1E All specialist teachers in gifted education should possess a certification/specialization or degree in gifted education.
	2.2M Any teacher whose primary responsibility for teaching includes gifted learners must have extensive expertise in gifted education.	2.2E Only teachers with advanced expertise in gifted education should have primary responsibility for the education of gifted learners.

3. School personnel require support for their specific efforts related to the education of gifted learners.

3.0M School personnel must be released from their professional duties to participate in staff development efforts in gifted education.

3.0E Approved staff development activities in gifted education should be funded at least in part by school districts or educational agencies.

4. The educational staff must be provided with time and other support for the preparation and development of the differentiated education plans, materials, curriculum.

4.0M School personnel must be allotted planning time to prepare for the differentiated education of gifted learners.

4.0E Regularly scheduled planning time (e.g., release time, summer pay, etc.) should be allotted to teachers for the development of differentiated educational programs and related resources.

Gifted Education Programming Criterion: Program Evaluation

Description: Program evaluation is the systematic study of the value and impact of services provided.

Guiding Principles		Minimum Standards		Exemplary Standards
1. An evaluation must be purposeful.	1.0M	Information collected must reflect the interests and needs of most of the constituency groups.	1.0E	Information collected should address pertinent questions raised by all constituency groups and should be responsive to the needs of all stakeholders.
2. An evaluation must be efficient and economic.	2.0M	School districts must provide sufficient resources for program evaluation.	2.0E	School districts should allocate adequate time, financial support, and personnel to conduct systematic program evaluation.
3. An evaluation must be conducted competently and ethically.	3.0M	Persons conducting the evaluation must be competent and trustworthy.	3.0E	Persons conducting the evaluation should possess an expertise in program evaluation in gifted education.
	3.1M	The program evaluation design must address whether or not services have reached intended goals.	3.1E	The evaluation design should report the strengths and weaknesses found in the program, as well as critical issues that might influence program services.
	3.2M	Instruments and procedures used for data collection must be valid and reliable for their intended use.	3.2E	Care should be taken to ensure that instruments with sufficient evidence of reliability and validity are used and that they are appropriate for varying age, developmental levels, gender, and diversity of the target population.
	3.3M	Ongoing formative and summative evaluation strategies must be used for substantive program improvement and development.	3.3E	Formative evaluations should be conducted regularly with summative evaluations occurring minimally every five years or more often as specified by state or local district policies.

3.4M Individual data must be held confidential.

3.4E All individuals who are involved in the evaluation process should be given the opportunity to verify information and the resulting interpretation.

4. The evaluation results must be made available through a written report.

4.0M Evaluation reports must present the evaluation results in a clear and cohesive format.

4.0E Evaluation reports should be designed to present results and encourage follow-through by stakeholders.

About the Authors

Mary S. Landrum, Ph.D., has taught in higher education for 10 years. Previously, she was an elementary and middle school teacher. Dr. Landrum is a member of the board of directors of the National Association for Gifted Children and won the Early Leader Award from that organization in 1997. Mary is coauthor of a staff development book published collaboratively by Prufrock Press, Inc., and the National Association for Gifted Children and has a new book on consultation and gifted education being published by Creative Learning Press.

Carolyn M. Callahan, Ph.D., professor in the Curry School of Education, University of Virginia is also associate director of the National Research Center on the Gifted and Talented. She teaches courses in the area of education of the gifted, and is executive director of the Summer Enrichment Program. Dr. Callahan has authored more than 130 articles, 25 book chapters and monographs in gifted education focusing on creativity, the identification of gifted students, program evaluation, and the issues faced by gifted females. Dr. Callahan has received recognition as Outstanding Faculty Member in the Commonwealth of Virginia and was awarded the Distinguished Scholar Award from the National Association for Gifted Children. She is a past-president of The Association for the Gifted and the National Association for Gifted Children. She also sits on the editorial boards of *Gifted Child Quarterly, Journal for the Education of the Gifted,* and *Roeper Review.*

Beverly D. Shaklee, Ed.D., is currently special assistant to the dean for teacher education and a full professor in teaching, leadership, and curriculum studies at Kent State University. She has served as chair of the Professional Development Division, co-chair of the President's Committee on Standards, and on the board of directors of the National Association for Gifted Children .

Gloria L. Cox is the director of talent development and advanced studies for the Charlotte-Mecklenburg Schools in Charlotte, NC. She previously coordinated gifted programs in Nebraska. She has served on the Nebraska State Advisory Board for Gifted Education and as an officer of the Nebraska Association for the Gifted. Mrs. Cox is the vice-chair of the Professional Development Division of the National Association for Gifted Children.

Mary Evans has been the principal at Cumberland Trace Elementary School for the past four years. Her school is designated as a Model Site in Gifted and Talented Education by the Kentucky Department of Education. Prior to joining the Cumberland Trace School staff, she was the program coordinator for The Center for Gifted Studies at Western Kentucky University. She is a past-president of the Kentucky Association for Gifted Education and is currently a doctoral candidate in the University of Louisville/Western Kentucky University Cooperative Doctoral Program.

Helen L. Nevitt, Ph.D., is director of special education for Maine School Administrative District No. 72 in Fryeburg. She supervises both special education and gifted education programs. Helen has served at several levels of education, elementary through higher education. She has taught courses in gifted education and coordinated a university Scholars Program. Her areas of scholarly interest are the socio-emotional functioning of gifted students and the recognition of gifted education among low socio-economic populations. She is active in the National Association for Gifted Children where she is currently the past-chair of the Counseling and Guidance Division.

Kimberley Chandler is the supervisor of enrichment programs in Amherst County, VA. She is a doctoral student at the College of William and Mary, where her concentration is gifted education administration. She is active in several NAGC divisions and edits the organizational newsletter for the Virginia Association for the Gifted. She was a recipient of the A. Harry Passow Classroom Teacher Scholarship in 1997.

Susan Hansford, Ph.D., is supervisor of advanced study and enrichment for North Olmsted City Schools in Ohio. She has been active in gifted education in Ohio since 1980, serving as a full-time coordinator of gifted education for the past 16 years. Dr. Hansford is past-president of the Consortium of Ohio Coordinators for Gifted, chair of NAGC's Professional Development Division, and is a member of the Ohio Advisory Council for Gifted Education. Dr. Hansford teaches gifted education courses at Kent State University and has been involved in research on the identification of underrepresented gifted populations: young gifted children, African American gifted children, and learning-disabled gifted children.

Aimee Bonar received her masters' in education in 2000 and is currently studying for a Ph.D. in school psychology. Her interests involve home/school collaboration and interventions for special education students in the secondary level.

Nicole Burge graduated with her bachelor of arts in psychology from Cleveland State University. She is currently enrolled at Kent State University in the school psychology program where she received her masters' of education. Ms. Burge aspires to work as a school psychologist and specialize in behavioral management and gifted education.

Jeanine M. Scally is currently pursuing an educational specialists degree at Kent State University in school psychology and will graduate in 2001. Her areas of interest include gifted education, early childhood education, and early intervention. Ms. Scally plans to gain some experience by working in the schools for a few years, and then returning to graduate school for a doctoral degree.